A promise is a promise

A promise is a promise

How God provides for his people

Roger Ellsworth

 EVANGELICAL PRESS

EVANGELICAL PRESS
12 Wooler Street, Darlington, Co. Durham, DL1 1RQ, England

© Evangelical Press 1996
First published 1996

British Library Cataloguing in Publication Data available

ISBN 0 85234 387 6

Printed and bound in Great Britain at the Bath Press

In memory of Immanuel's beloved deacon
and my dear friend and soulmate
Lester Auten

Contents

Acknowledgements

As always, I profoundly appreciate the assistance of Beth Bozeman, Sheila Ketteman and Susan Bailie in making these chapters possible.

I am also grateful to my wife Sylvia for her encouragement and support and to the congregation of Immanuel Baptist Church for joyfully walking with me through many of these promises. I am also indebted to Pat Stewart and Chuck Todd for sharing valuable insights with me.

Introduction

We all know what a promise is. It is the announcement of an intention. It is when someone declares he or she intends to do something, or to give something.

There are two categories of promises: the promises of men and the promises of God. The former type includes promises we make to ourselves, promises we make to each other and the promises we make to God. In the latter category, there are the promises made by the three persons of the Trinity to each other and the promises God has made to us. There is nothing especially spectacular about the promises of men, but when it comes to the promises of God — that is a different story!

Promises between the three persons of the Trinity

It may be somewhat surprising to some to hear of promises made between the three persons of the Trinity, but Scripture gives us glimpses into this reality. God the Father, God the Son and God the Holy Spirit entered into covenant with each other before the world began to map out the plan of redemption. The three persons of the Holy Trinity knew beforehand that man would sin, and they set in place a plan by which to redeem a great multitude of sinners. This plan consisted of the Father choosing a people for himself, the Son becoming a man and purchasing redemption for those chosen and the Holy Spirit applying that purchased redemption to their individual hearts.

The first promises ever made, then, were by the Father to the Son. In his *Systematic Theology*, L. Berkhof enumerates these promises as follows:

1. The Father would prepare a human body for the Son that would be uncontaminated by sin (Heb. 10:5).

2. The Father would endow him with the necessary gifts and graces for the performance of his task.

3. The Father would support him in the performance of his work, would deliver him from the power of death and would thus enable him to destroy the dominion of Satan and to establish the kingdom of God.

4. The Father would enable him, as a reward for his accomplished work, to send out the Holy Spirit for the formation of his spiritual body, and for the instruction, guidance and protection of the church.

5. The Father would give unto him a numerous seed in reward for his accomplished work, a seed so numerous that it would be a multitude which no man could number.

6. The Father would commit to him all power in heaven and on earth for the government of the world and of his church, and would finally reward him as Mediator with the glory which he as the Son of God had with the Father before the world was.[1]

Puritan Thomas Boston offers a different classification of these same promises. He says the Lord Jesus received essentially three promises from the Father. First was the promise of *assistance in* his work. Then there was the promise of *acceptance of* his work. Finally, there was the promise of *reward for* his work.[2]

The promises God made to Christ are only some of the promises in this category. There are also the promises Christ made to the Father and to the Holy Spirit (to come into this world and provide atonement for all who believe), and the promises the Holy Spirit made to the Father and to the Son (to come into this world to exalt Christ and to apply his finished work of redemption to individual hearts).

The promises of God to men

That brings us to the second part of this category of God's promises, those this book is concerned with — the promises of God to men. Think about it: God has made promises to men! It is an awesome and compelling thought.

First, we must make sure we have some appreciation of who God is. He is the sovereign Creator and Ruler of all things. He is perfect in wisdom, unlimited in power and resplendent with glory. He sees all and knows all. He is holy and righteous.

And then we must make sure we know who we are. First, *we are creatures*. God, who created all things, has created us. Secondly, *we are fallen creatures*. We are not as God made us. The distance between Creator and creature is great enough, but the distance between us and God has been made inexplicably vast by virtue of our sinfulness.

Now, with these things firmly etched in our minds, let us step back and view these promises once again. God has made promises to us! He was under no obligation to us at all, but he has freely put himself under an obligation to us by making promises to us.

'The Christian's God is a promising God.' So says one of the great Puritans, Robert Traill.[3] There could be no Christianity without this. Christianity exists because God has made his promises.

The Christian is one who *trusts* God, but what would there be to trust, what would there be to depend on, if God had not made promises to us? The apostle Paul says, 'So then faith comes by hearing, and hearing by the Word of God' (Rom. 10:17).

The Christian *seeks to obey the laws of God*, but what would be the incentive for obedience if there were no promises from God?

The Christian *prays* because he has promises from God. Traill says, 'The main thing in prayer is to put God in mind of the promise. The great work of Christians is to turn promises into prayers, and God will turn both into performance.'[4]

The Christian *has hope for a glorious future* in heaven. Where does he get such hope? From the promises of God!

The Christian *is called to demonstrate life at its best.* He is to be a model of peace and joy. How can he do so? By trusting the promises of God!

All of these things ought to give us pause. The truth is that we Christians are sadly lacking in many of these areas. It would appear that a number of spiritual viruses and 'bugs' have taken hold of us. There is a lack of vibrancy and bounce in most of us. There is little that could be considered as a passion for God, but there is much infatuation with the world's thinking and doing. Discouragement and weariness with the Lord's work appear to be running at floodtide. The promises of God can help us. They have the remarkable ability to purge the soul of what ails it. They can serve as a tonic to refresh and reinvigorate sagging, dragging spirits.

Another Puritan, Richard Sibbes, writes, 'God supports the souls and spirits of his children with promises, to arm them against temptations on the right hand and on the left...'[5]

The purpose of these chapters is to parade some of the promises of God before the reader so that he or she might find the strength and support they are designed to give.

But where to begin? Charles Spurgeon says of God's promises, 'Why, here is a grand granaryful! Who can sort them all out?'[6]

The task is indeed daunting, but the attempt must be made. The following division has commended itself to me as a helpful way to approach the many promises of God. First, we shall look at Christ and the promises. After that, we shall come to the promises themselves. There are so many that it is necessary to do some categorizing or structuring. But what structure is the most serviceable?

As I reflected on the pilgrim status of the Christian in this world, it occurred to me that there are promises that start us on our journey, promises that sustain us on our journey and promises for the end of the journey. The structure I have adopted is, therefore, as follows: promises for setting off, promises for the journey and promises for the journey's end.

It is my hope that our journey through these promises will fill our hearts with a fresh sense of amazement and wonder at our promising God, will fire them with determination to reflect his glory and promote his kingdom and will provide the 'heart-lift' so many Christians are desperately needing these days.

Section I
Christ and the promises

Any study of the promises of God to mankind must begin with the Lord Jesus Christ, and that for the following reasons: first, Christ is himself the greatest of all God's promises; secondly, if it were not for him, we should all be in a state of alienation from God and should not have any promises from him at all.

In connecting the promises with Christ, Robert Traill says he is 'the channel wherein they run'.[1] Traill explains by saying all the promises of God are 'in and through Jesus Christ',[2] and adds this word of caution and warning: 'That man looks with a bad eye upon any of the promises of God, that does not see Christ in them; and they do not see Christ rightly, unless they see all the promises in him.'[3]

The chapters that follow examine the connections between Christ and the promises of God. As we look at them, we shall be able to glimpse what Andrew Gray calls 'a threefold sight of Christ'.[4]

First, we shall be amazed at the sight of 'the boundless and condescending love of Christ',[5] that would compel him to lay aside all the trappings of glory and stoop so low as to take our humanity unto himself for ever. What possessed him to do such a thing? It was all for the purpose of plucking us from the pit of sin and elevating us to that high position of being adopted into God's own family. There is no greater love.

As we examine Christ's role in the promises, we shall also stand amazed at the sight of his 'faithfulness and unchangeableness'.[6]

Our plans are characterized by adjustment and change. What we plan today has to be modified tomorrow, but it is not so with God. The plans he formed long ago were so perfectly and minutely fulfilled by Christ that we can speak Isaiah's words to the Lord: 'Your counsels of old are faithfulness and truth' (Isa. 25:1).

That leads, in turn, to the sight of the 'omnipotency'[7] of Christ. Plans formed long ago can only be perfectly carried out if the one who formed them has perfect power.

God's people sorely need this threefold sight of Christ. Casual observation of the current religious scene yields the conclusion that many are serving a severely truncated Christ. And they are the losers. A miniature Christ will never elicit a robust faith, and anaemic faith will never stir us to great exploits for God or enable us to experience peace and joy in the midst of our circumstances.

1.
The first grand promise

Genesis 3:15

Richard Sibbes says, 'The promise of Christ is the first grand promise, that he should be made man...'[1] He was referring, of course, to the words of Genesis 3:15:

> And I will put enmity
> Between you and the woman,
> And between your seed and her Seed;
> He shall bruise your head,
> And you shall bruise his heel.

These words were addressed by the Lord to Satan after his temptation of Eve had led her and Adam into disobedience, but they were spoken in the hearing of Adam and Eve and primarily for their benefit.

The promise needed

The main result of Adam's disobedience was alienation from God. Before they sinned, Adam and Eve knew God intimately, but their sin changed all that. No part of Adam and Eve was left unaffected by their sin. Their minds, which understood God's truth at the first, were darkened by sin. Their hearts, or affections, which originally loved and embraced God, were degraded. Their wills, which once freely chose to serve God, were now deadened.

Let us never forget that what sin did to Adam and Eve, it did to all of us. Yes, the Bible tells us Adam was not just an ordinary man who acted for himself; he was, in fact, the representative head of the whole human race. What he did counted for us all. When he disobeyed God's law, we all disobeyed it. His act was our act. We all come into this world, therefore, with a sinful nature. Darkened minds, degraded affections, deadened wills — this is the legacy our father has left us.

The promise given

God would have been perfectly justified in washing his hands of his fallen creatures. After Adam and Eve sinned, he could simply have walked away, and no one could have lifted so much as a single finger in accusation against him. But, in grace that boggles the mind, God refused to walk away. He came to the Garden of Eden where Adam and Eve were hiding, sought them out and revealed to them his plan to rescue them from their spiritual death and alienation and restore them to fellowship with himself.

This plan centred round a person. In his words to Satan, God refers to 'her Seed', that is, the Seed of the woman. In other words, God was promising to send a man. He was essentially saying to Satan, 'You brought sin into the human race through a man, and I am going to provide a way for sinners to be forgiven of their sins through a man.'

That reference to the 'Seed of the woman' makes it clear that the man whom God promised to send would be no ordinary man. In Scripture descent is always reckoned through the male line, but the man God would send to provide redemption for sinners would spring from a human mother, but not from a human father. Whom would God send to do this marvellous work? His own Son, the Lord Jesus Christ, who would be born of the virgin Mary.

Furthermore, God promised that there would be continual hostility between Satan, and all who belong to him, and this 'Seed of the woman'. The hatred of Satan for Christ would eventually culminate in Satan's bruising the heel of Christ. But in the course of his bruising Christ's heel, Satan's own head would be crushed.

This is nothing less than a beautiful picture of the cross of Christ. There it looked as if Satan had won a great victory. He had marshalled all his forces and had succeeded in getting evil men to nail Jesus to a cross. But what appeared to be a mighty victory for Satan was in reality his undoing. Christ's death on the cross actually purchased salvation for the people God had promised to give him and dealt the death-blow to Satan's kingdom. John Stallings captures the essence of it in these memorable lines:

See my Jesus on the cross, the people crying.
Looking on a man would think it tragedy.
But what the world could not see
When they nailed him to that tree,
It would break the chains of sin's captivity.

The promise pictured

In addition to giving this promise in the hearing of Adam and Eve, God proceeded to give them a picture of the redemption his Son would provide. He did this by killing animals and making coats of skin with which to cover Adam and Eve (Gen. 3:21).

After their sin, Adam and Eve had made fig-leaf coverings
for themselves but, by killing those animals and making those
coverings, God rejected their own attempts to cover themselves. In essence, God was saying several things to them:

    1. In order to stand in my holy presence you must be
clothed.
    2. There is absolutely nothing you can do to clothe
yourselves acceptably.
    3. I myself will provide what is necessary for you to
stand in my presence.
    4. What I provide to clothe you and make you
acceptable in my sight must involve the shedding of
blood.

Why was this shedding of blood necessary? God had said
the penalty for sin would be death. Adam and Eve had sinned,
and now the penalty must be paid. Either they had to pay it
themselves, or someone else had to pay it for them. By killing
those animals there in the garden, God instituted the principle
of substitution and pictured the essential nature of what Christ
would do to provide redemption. The animals were innocent
of sin, but they died so that Adam and Eve might be covered.
The Lord Jesus Christ would also be innocent of sin, but he
would die in the place of sinners and, in so doing, would
provide a covering for sinners.

The promise reinforced

From the moment God killed those animals, this principle of
substitution became the central, guiding theme of the Old
Testament. All those who looked forward in faith to the

coming substitute, Jesus Christ, were forgiven of their sins and covered with the garment of righteousness.

Substitution was the issue in the story of Cain and Abel. Abel believed the Word of God, the word that had been first delivered to his parents and through them to him, and he came to God on the basis of the shed blood of an innocent substitute. Cain, on the other hand, refused to come in God's way. Abel was accepted and Cain was rejected.

This concept of substitution was reinforced and confirmed by God in the life of Abraham. Abraham was commanded by God to offer up his son Isaac, but God intervened and provided a substitute for Isaac.

God also reinforced this teaching of substitution for the whole nation of Israel when he delivered them from slavery in Egypt. Each Israelite was to slay a lamb and put its blood at the top and on each side of his door. When God's angel of judgement passed over Egypt, all those in houses marked with the blood of that substitute were saved from death.

When the nation of Israel was safely out of Egypt, God made the sacrificing of innocent animals the centrepiece of their worship. What was the point of it all? In sacrificing those animals the people were looking forward in faith to the coming of the perfect substitute who would finally make complete atonement for sin.

We also find this theme of substitution in the preaching of the prophets. Isaiah, for example, declared that the coming Messiah would be 'led as a lamb to the slaughter', and through that act of substitution would 'justify many' (Isa. 53:7,11).

The idea of forgiveness of sin through the death of an innocent substitute runs throughout the entire Old Testament. It is the great, unifying theme of the Old Testament.

The promise fulfilled

Finally, it all culminated in the coming of Christ. Paul puts it like this in Galatians 4:4: 'But when the fulness of the time had come, God sent forth his Son, born of a woman...'

The animals of the Old Testament could not actually provide atonement for sin. They could only symbolize or picture atonement. How was it possible for Jesus to do what these animal sacrifices could only faintly picture? The answer is that Jesus was a man himself and could, therefore, represent men. But he was more than a man. He was God in human flesh. Because he was God, he could represent more than one man. On top of all that, he was sinless. Because he had no sins of his own to pay for, he could pay for the sins of others.

This he did, in keeping with the promise of God, on Calvary's cross. In the coming of Jesus 'the grand promise' was fulfilled. The great question is not whether God has kept his promise to send a Saviour for sinners. He has! The Lord Jesus Christ is the fulfilment of that promise. The great question is whether we have received the Christ provided by God as the only sufficient sacrifice for sinners.

2.
Old Testament promises fulfilled by Christ

Luke 24:27,44

God gave Adam and Eve the promise that the Messiah would come, but he did not leave it at that. He proceeded to give several detailed promises and pictures of this coming Messiah. These promises and pictures are so numerous that we can go so far as to say the whole Old Testament is about the Lord Jesus Christ. How do we know this to be true? Because he himself affirmed it.

Christ claims to be the fulfilment

On the day of his resurrection, he joined a couple of his disciples on their journey from Jerusalem to Emmaus. These men were befuddled and confused. They were convinced that Jesus was indeed the Messiah, but they had not allowed for the possibility of his being crucified (Luke 24:17-21). In addition to that, they found themselves bewildered over the reports that he had risen from the grave (Luke 24:22-24).

The Lord Jesus reproached them for their bewilderment by assuring them that all that had happened was nothing less than the fulfilment of Old Testament prophecies. Luke puts it in these words: 'And beginning at Moses and all the Prophets, he expounded to them in all the Scriptures the things concerning himself' (Luke 24:27).

Later that evening the Lord Jesus appeared to a group of his disciples in Jerusalem. On that occasion, the Lord said, 'These are the words which I spoke to you while I was still with you, that all things must be fulfilled which were written in the Law of Moses and the Prophets and the Psalms concerning me' (Luke 24:44).

We have, then, two explicit statements from the Lord himself that he is the subject and focus of every part of the Old Testament.

Matthew and Luke proclaim Christ as the fulfilment

When we begin to examine the Gospel accounts of the Lord Jesus and compare them with the Old Testament prophecies, we are amazed at how precisely he fulfilled them.

Think for a moment about the birth of Christ. Matthew's account repeatedly emphasizes that it all happened in precise fulfilment of prophecy. His first two chapters contain the phrase 'that it might be fulfilled' a total of three times (1:22; 2:15,23). They also contain the phrases, 'Then was fulfilled...' (2:17) and 'Thus it is written by the prophet...' (2:5).

What Old Testament prophecies were fulfilled on that occasion?

The virgin birth

Matthew first cites the virgin birth (1:22-23). Joseph and Mary had not yet married when Mary 'was found' to be with child (1:18). While Joseph was pondering these things, an angel appeared to him with the astounding news that Mary was 'with child of the Holy Spirit' (1:18,20). She had conceived through an act of the Holy Spirit of God (Luke 1:35).

This act of the Holy Spirit was for the purpose of bringing into this world the Son of God so that he might 'save his people from their sins' (Matt. 1:21). And it was in keeping with what the prophet Isaiah had declared centuries before: 'Behold, the virgin shall conceive and bear a Son, and call his name Immanuel...' (Isa. 7:14; Matt. 1:23).

Was Jesus born of a virgin? The evidence says he was. Keep in mind that Luke joined Matthew in affirming the virgin birth. These Gospels were written only a few years after Jesus' death. Many who had been closely associated with Joseph and Mary and, therefore, knew the circumstances of Jesus' birth, were still alive when these Gospels began to circulate. In all probability, Mary was still alive at this time. All of these people and Mary herself would have set the record straight if the accounts of a virgin birth were mere fabrications.

Luke's account of the virgin birth is especially noteworthy because he was a physician. His training would have made him extremely sceptical of a virgin birth, but he gives us the more detailed account of it!

The place of the Messiah's birth

Another fulfilment of Old Testament prophecy cited by Matthew has to do with the place of the Messiah's birth. The Old Testament said it would be 'Bethlehem' (Micah 5:2). All the religious leaders convened by Herod readily agreed — Bethlehem was the place where the Messiah was to be born (Matt. 2:4-6). No one, no matter how sceptical and antagonistic towards Christianity, even bothers to dispute the fact that Jesus was born in Bethlehem.

This fulfilment was no small matter. Joseph and Mary were from Nazareth, which was over seventy miles north of the village of Bethlehem, a very significant distance in those days.

How did Joseph and Mary happen to be in Bethlehem on the very night that the Lord Jesus was born?

The answer is supplied for us by Luke: 'And it came to pass … that a decree went out from Caesar Augustus that all the world should be registered. This census first took place while Quirinius was governing Syria. So all went to be registered, everyone to his own city. And Joseph also went up from Galilee, out of the city of Nazareth, into Judea, to the city of David, which is called Bethlehem, because he was of the house and lineage of David, to be registered with Mary, his betrothed wife, who was with child' (Luke 2:1-5).

Out of all the times when Caesar could have issued a decree for everyone to return to his home town to be registered, he 'just happened' to choose the date that would bring Joseph and Mary to Bethlehem just at the time when Mary was to give birth to Jesus and fulfil Micah's prophecy. God's timing is exquisite!

These two fulfilments — the manner of Jesus' birth and the place of it — are impressive enough, but, as we have noted, they are only two of the fulfilments cited by Matthew.

The killing of the children and flight into Egypt

After Jesus was born, Herod the king was enraged over the thought of having a rival king on his hands, and ordered all the male children under two years of age to be put to death in Bethlehem and the surrounding area (2:16). Matthew also declares that to be a fulfilment of prophecy (2:18).

Joseph and Mary fled from Herod's wrath into Egypt and, after Herod's death, returned to Nazareth. All of this fulfilled the Old Testament prophecies found in Numbers 24:8; Hosea 11:1 and Jeremiah 31:15 (see Matt. 2:13-15,19-23).

The life of Christ

After his account of the birth of Christ, Matthew launches into a description of the life of Christ, and he again constantly employs that phrase 'that it might be fulfilled' (4:14; 8:17;12:17;13:14,35; 21:4; 27:35).

The first of these references deals with the Lord Jesus coming to the region of Zebulun and Naphtali, a move which fulfilled the prophecy found in Isaiah 9:1-2.

The second deals with Jesus' healing ministry, which fulfilled the prophecy found in Isaiah 53:4.

The third also deals with the ministry of Jesus and pronounces it a fulfilment of Isaiah 42:1-4 and Isaiah 49:3.

The verses in Matthew 13 deal with Jesus' teaching in parables and declare that also to be a fulfilment of a cluster of Old Testament prophecies (Ps. 78:2; Isa. 6:9-10; Zech. 7:11).

Matthew wraps up the life of Christ by affirming that the triumphal entry of Jesus into Jerusalem was a distinct fulfilment of Zechariah 9:9.

The death and resurrection of Christ

Then Matthew takes us to the crucifixion of Christ and affirms that the dividing of his garments was the fulfilment of Psalm 22:18.

But Matthew's explicit statements that the birth, life and death of Christ fulfilled prophecy are only the tip of the iceberg. We should keep in mind that Matthew passes by some of Jesus' fulfilments of prophecy without explicitly calling them fulfilments. Take the crucifixion of Jesus for a moment. Matthew mentions that Jesus was given 'sour wine mingled with gall' to drink (27:34), but he does not say that this was a fulfilment of Psalm 69:21.

Neither does Matthew mention the resurrection of Jesus as a fulfilment of prophecy. He left that for Luke to do in his account of the experiences of the early church. And Luke did it forcefully. Acts 2:25-31 affirms Jesus' resurrection to be a fulfilment of Psalm 16:8-11. Acts 13:33-35 affirms it to be a fulfilment of Psalm 2:7 and Isaiah 55:3 as well as Psalm 16:10.

The preaching and teaching of the early church

Luke also makes mention of many other prophecies Jesus fulfilled and makes it clear that fulfilled prophecy played a prominent part in the preaching and teaching of the early church (Acts 1:20; 2:16-21,34-35; 3:22-26; 4:11,25-26, etc.).

We should keep in mind as well that Matthew and Luke were not alone in emphasizing the element of fulfilled prophecy in the birth, life and death of Christ. It is a recurring theme in the New Testament.

Josh McDowell, in his *Evidence That Demands a Verdict*, maintains that Jesus fulfilled over three hundred prophecies and proceeds to show how he fulfilled sixty-one of these.[1]

The importance of fulfilment

Why is this matter of fulfilled prophecy so important? There can be no doubt about the answer to that question. It proved beyond any shadow of doubt that the baby in Bethlehem's stable was no ordinary baby. He was, in fact, what the Bible declares him to be, God in human flesh.

This is, of course, the uniform testimony of the apostles. Paul puts this immense truth in the tiniest of packages: 'God was in Christ' (2 Cor. 5:19).

The apostle John, who went about with the Lord Jesus during his earthly ministry, summarizes it in this way: 'And the Word became flesh and dwelt among us, and we beheld his glory, the glory as of the only begotten of the Father, full of grace and truth' (John 1:14).

Yes, Jesus was a real man, but as John and the other disciples closely observed him they could see that he was more than a man. They could see flickering through that real humanity the glory of God himself. John and the other apostles would have readily agreed with Charles Wesley's immortal lines:

Veiled in flesh the Godhead see,
Hail, the incarnate Deity!

That which the disciples of Jesus saw shining through the humanity of Jesus compelled them to worship him as nothing less than God himself.

As we read the Gospel accounts of Jesus' life, and as we see in those accounts the careful fulfilment of prophecy after prophecy, we can see that same glory of God shining in the life of Christ. The only proper way to respond to such glory is to fall before it in adoration, praise and submission, saying with Wesley, 'Hail the incarnate Deity!'

3.
Christ fulfilling Isaiah 53

Isaiah 53:1-12

It is almost impossible to talk about Christ fulfilling the promises of the Old Testament without dealing with this much-loved chapter. The New Testament writers recognized this passage as one of the greatest prophecies of Christ and referred to it or quoted it several times.

This chapter constitutes part of one of the four 'Servant Songs' found in the latter half of Isaiah (42:1-9; 49:1-7; 50:4-11; 52:13 - 53:12). While these songs were in some measure fulfilled in the history of the nation of Israel, their ultimate fulfilment is quite obviously to be found in Christ.

The 53rd chapter of Isaiah contains promises regarding the life of Christ, his death and the results of his death.

Promises about the life of Christ

The prophecies regarding the life of Christ (vv. 2-3) are essentially of two types. First, we are told there would be nothing especially attractive about him to those who rejected him; but, secondly, those who were to receive him would see him from a radically different perspective.

This is quite easily demonstrated from the Gospel accounts of the life of Jesus. The Jews had all kinds of marvellous ideas about what their Messiah would be like, and Jesus failed at every point to live up to their expectations.

For one thing, the Jews expected the Messiah to come from a noble background, but Jesus sprang from very common, unimpressive surroundings, like a 'root out of dry ground' (v. 2). He grew up in a humble carpenter's shop in Nazareth. What a combination — a humble trade in a humble village! This is hardly the stuff from which one might expect a Messiah to be made!

The Jews also seem to have expected their Messiah to be unusually attractive and striking in appearance, but Jesus came without 'form or comeliness' (v. 2). How do we know this to be true? With all the New Testament tells us about Jesus, there is not so much as a single indication that he was anything but very ordinary in his appearance.

The Jews also expected the Messiah to be something of a joyful extrovert who would easily win a great following. But Jesus proved to be a 'man of sorrows' who was 'acquainted with grief' and 'despised and rejected by men'.

The sorrow experienced by Jesus is abundantly evident in the Gospels (Luke 19:41-44; 22:44; John 11:35), as are the spitefulness and rejection he received at the hands of men (John 1:11; 5:40; 6:60,66). Much of this sorrow was due to his bearing the griefs and sorrows of those around him. Matthew specifically declares the healing ministry of Christ to be nothing less than the Messiah bearing the griefs and sorrows of a sin-laden humanity (Matt. 8:17).

Along with Isaiah's prophecy of how most would view the life of Jesus, we also see in these verses how those who believed in him would perceive it. The unbelieving Jews of Jesus' day saw nothing in his birth or person that was special, but the eye of faith recognizes that, even in his humble surroundings and common life, Jesus was growing up as 'a tender plant' before God the Father (v. 2). The Father had sent

him on a special mission, and each day he was pleased to see
the steady development of Jesus and his faithful fulfilment of
his mission.

Promises about the death of Christ

The major part of Isaiah 53 is reserved for the death of Christ
(vv. 4-12). Christ's fulfilment of these prophecies is easily
demonstrated.

Consider the following details of Isaiah's prophecy. He
says the Messiah would:

> be wounded for our transgressions, bruised for our
> iniquities and receive 'stripes' for our healing (v. 5);
> be silent before his accusers (v. 7);
> be buried in a rich man's tomb (v. 9);
> be innocent of any wrong-doing (v. 9);
> be numbered with transgressors (v. 12);
> make intercession for transgressors (v. 12).
> All of these things would be in keeping with God's
> plan: God would smite him (v. 4), lay our iniquities upon
> him (v. 6) and bruise him (v. 10).

The writers of the New Testament vigorously assert and
affirm that each one of those seven prophecies found its
fulfilment in Christ.

> Peter says the Lord Jesus 'bore our sins in his own
> body on the tree' and then specifically quotes Isaiah's
> phrase: 'by whose stripes you were healed' (1 Peter
> 2:24).
> Matthew specifically states that Jesus was silent
> before his accusers (Matt. 26:63).

Matthew also points out that Jesus was buried in the tomb of a rich man (Matt. 27:57-60).

Peter asserts that Jesus was innocent of any wrong-doing, and claims this to be a fulfilment of Isaiah's words (1 Peter 2:22).

Mark declares that Jesus' crucifixion between two thieves was a fulfilment of Isaiah's prophecy that Messiah would be numbered with the transgressors (Mark 15:28).

Luke mentions that Jesus prayed for those who crucified him, an obvious fulfilment of Isaiah's claim that the Messiah would make intercession for transgressors (Luke 23:34).

Jesus himself asserted on numerous occasions that all he did was in keeping with the plan of God (John 5:30; 8:42; 18:11).

Promises regarding the results of Christ's death

Isaiah's prophecy carries us beyond the life and death of Christ to the results. The phrase, 'He shall prolong his days' (v. 10), points us to the resurrection of Christ. The death of Christ was not the end of him. On the third day, he arose from the grave and now shouts triumphantly across the ages: 'I am alive for evermore' (Rev. 1:18).

Isaiah also prophesied that the Messiah's death would not be in vain, but it would be the means of many being justified (v. 11). That word 'justified' is a legal term. To be justified means a judge has pronounced one to be righteous and not liable to any penalty. It is the opposite of condemnation.

The Bible tells us God is holy and must judge sin. But he is also gracious and loving and desires, therefore, to forgive sinners. The great dilemma for God, if we may put it in this way, was how to judge sin and at the same time justify guilty sinners. Justice demanded that he do the former. He had pledged to judge sin, and had he refused to do so he would have compromised his own holy character. But grace, on the other hand, demanded that God find a way for the sinner to go free.

The cross is God's answer to the demands of his justice and his grace. Justice was satisfied there in that Jesus received the penalty it demanded, but grace was also satisfied in that those who cast themselves on Christ's payment for sin do not have to pay the penalty themselves. It has been paid for them by Jesus Christ.

This leads us to one more aspect of Isaiah's prophecy, namely, that the Messiah would be satisfied with what his death would accomplish. True believers are the seed of Christ. They are the results of Christ's death. The Father gave them to him in eternity past, and by his substitutionary death he paid for their sins and purchased them for himself.

We have, therefore, in every aspect of Christ's life and death many striking answers to Isaiah's 53rd chapter. But what is the point of tracking these parallels? Is it only so we can marvel at them? It goes much farther than that. Christ's detailed fulfilment of Isaiah's prophecy proves beyond debate that he is the Redeemer promised by God to Adam and Eve.

It also does something else for us. It proves God was so scrupulous about fulfilling in and through Christ all the prophecies he made to Isaiah that we can rest assured he will fulfil all his other promises.

4.
God's promises in Christ

2 Corinthians 1:20

'For all the promises of God in him are Yes, and in him Amen, to the glory of God through us.'

These words are part of Paul's response to a charge that had been levelled against him by the Corinthians. He had been unable to make an intended visit to the church in Corinth, and that had caused some to level the charge of fickleness against him. In other words, they took Paul's change of plans as proof that he was unreliable. They were saying that when Paul said 'yes' he really meant 'no', and vice versa. Paul responded to this accusation with the words of our text. He simply affirmed that he belonged lock, stock and barrel, to the one who was faithful to God. Paul could not serve a faithful Christ without being faithful himself.

In defending himself against this charge of fickleness, Paul reveals two very important and significant things about the promises of God. First, the promises of God are all 'in Christ'; and secondly, the promises of God in Christ are all 'Yes' and 'Amen'.

What does Paul mean by saying the promises of God are 'in Christ'? What are we to understand by this? In what sense can it be said that God's promises are 'in Christ'? Richard Sibbes says, 'All promises are either Christ himself, or by Christ, or from Christ, or for Christ.'[1]

We might say, then, that every promise of God has some connection to the Lord Jesus Christ. This should not surprise us. On the day of his resurrection, the Lord Jesus travelled with two of his disciples from Jerusalem to Emmaus. Luke tells us that as they walked along the Lord Jesus 'expounded to them in all the Scriptures the things concerning himself' (Luke 24:27).

We find the promises of God in Scripture, and Scripture is all about Jesus Christ. He is the subject and the focus of it and is, therefore, the subject and the focus of all the promises of God.

We have already considered Christ himself as the greatest of all the promises and have noted some of the prophecies that were fulfilled by his birth, his life and his death. Let's go on now to consider the other connections between Christ and God's promises. We shall use the phrases suggested by Richard Sibbes as a guide.

Promises by Christ

Sibbes says God's promises come 'by Christ'. This means Christ is the channel or the agent through which God gives his people promises.

People today do not much care for this teaching, but it is emphatically clear in Scripture that we have absolutely no standing before God, nor can we expect to receive anything from him, except in and through the Lord Jesus Christ. He is, to use another phrase from Sibbes, the one 'that knits heaven and earth together'.[2] Take Christ out of the picture and we have absolutely no dealings with God at all.

The apostle Paul powerfully states this truth in these words: 'For there is one God and one Mediator between God and men, the Man Christ Jesus' (1 Tim. 2:5). The word 'mediator'

signifies one who comes in the middle to stand between parties
at variance and effect reconciliation. According to Scripture,
God and man are the parties at variance. God is the offended
party. The sin that Adam brought into our race is an affront to
God. It is nothing less than the creature asserting himself
against the Creator and essentially saying, 'I don't want you to
be God. I want to be God.' Sin is, therefore, no mere trifling
matter. It is a shaking of the fist in front of God's face. It is
enmity towards God.

Modern men and women have great difficulty in understanding the seriousness of sin. They cannot understand why
God does not just dismiss it as the foolish prank of naughty
children. Why are people so casual about sin? Because they
fail to see the nature of God. The Bible tells us God is a holy
and just God. His very character demands that he judge sin. For
him to ignore sin would amount to his denying who he is. This
he cannot do. Once we understand the holiness of God, we
have no trouble seeing why we cannot receive anything from
his hand as long as we are in our sins.

Here, then, is the great question, the question of the ages:
how can a guilty sinner ever stand clean and guiltless before
a holy God? And the answer is to be found in that word
'mediator'. Someone had to come between us and God and
bring peace and reconciliation. The Lord Jesus Christ has done
this. He is the Mediator between guilty sinners and a holy God.
He has made it possible for us to be at peace with God. How?
As we have already noted, he stood in the sinner's stead as a
substitute and took the penalty that God's justice demanded.

Now here is the glorious thing: God's justice demands
payment for sin once, and once that payment is made, it is
completely and fully satisfied. When Jesus Christ stood in my
stead and bore the wrath of God on my behalf, the justice of
God was satisfied once and for all. God does not now demand
that I pay for the very same sins Christ has already paid for.

The familiar lines of Augustus Toplady put it so well:

If thou hast my discharge fully procured,
And freely in my room endured
The whole of wrath divine;
Payment God cannot twice demand—
First at my bleeding Surety's hand,
And then again at mine.

Now that Christ has served as Mediator and removed the sin that had put us at variance with God, we can receive God's blessings and his promises. It is all by Christ.

Promise from Christ

Sibbes also says God's promises are 'from Christ'. With this phrase we come to a slightly different emphasis. God's promises are 'by' Christ in the sense that he removed the enmity between his people and God and made it possible for them to receive his promises. But the word 'from' implies that Christ himself is the giver of these promises to us. God, as it were, gives the promises to him, and he receives them on our behalf and gives them to us. Sibbes says, 'All the promises of good to us are made to Christ, and conveyed from Christ to us...'[3]

A. A. Hodge writes, 'The purchased benefits of the covenant are placed in Christ's hand, to be bestowed upon his people as free and sovereign gifts.'[4]

Just as God made Adam the first representative head of a humanity, the whole human race, and we received from him all that he did in that capacity; so he has made Christ the second representative head of a humanity — all those who receive him as Saviour and Lord — and they receive from him all he has done for them in that capacity.

The apostle Paul makes this point in his letter to the Galatians. He says, 'Now to Abraham and his Seed were the promises made. He does not say, "And to seeds," as of many, but as of one, "And to your Seed," who is Christ' (Gal. 3:16).

Paul's teaching is clear. God's promises are made, not to many people ('seeds'), but rather to one, and one alone (the 'Seed'). That one is none other than Christ himself. All God's promises are made to him, and him alone, as the head of his people. His people, then, share in these promises simply because he has received them from God on their behalf.

That word 'from' can also take us to another level. Not only does it mean the Lord Jesus gives to us the promises of God; it may also be taken to mean he gives us the power to meet the conditions that are attached to some of these promises. Andrew Gray writes, 'Christ giveth us strength to obey the condition that is annexed to the promises; and Christ infuseth habitual grace in us, by which we may be helped to exercise faith upon the promises: so that ... if Christ doth not help us, we would never believe a promise.'[5]

Promises for Christ

That brings us to Sibbes' final phrase — 'for Christ'. What is God's purpose in it all? Why did he determine that his promises should be purchased by Christ? Why did he determine to give his promises to Christ as the head of his people?

The answer is given by Paul. He says of Christ: 'And he is the head of the body, the church, who is the beginning, the firstborn from the dead, that in all things he may have the preeminence' (Col. 1:18).

In his letter to the Philippians, the apostle says of Christ: 'Therefore God also has highly exalted him and given him the name which is above every name, that at the name of Jesus every knee should bow, of those in heaven, and of those on earth, and of those under the earth, and that every tongue should confess that Jesus Christ is Lord, to the glory of God the Father' (Phil. 2:9-11).

God's grand purpose in centring everything on Christ is that Christ might have the pre-eminence in all things, and that in Christ having pre-eminence God himself may be glorified.

Christ himself is the greatest promise of all. The promises are by Christ. The promises are from Christ. The promises are for Christ. It is all Christ!

The importance of being Christ-centred

What effect should these things have upon us? They should make us ask ourselves some very searching and probing questions. First, we should each ask if we are truly in Christ. This is the most important and pressing of all questions. In Christ we receive all the promises of God, but apart from Christ we are strangers to these things.

If we are in Christ, we must ask ourselves some other questions. Do we realize to the degree that we should how much we owe Christ? Are we firmly holding to the truth as it is in Christ? Are we marvelling at what Christ has done for us? Are we aflame with love for Christ? Are we Christ-centred in our thinking and doing? Is our worship Christ-centred, or do we come to worship seeking to be entertained? Are we sharing Christ with others?

The crying need of this hour is for the church to realize afresh that she owes all to Christ. This will purge her life and reinvigorate her testimony.

5.
Christ: the guarantee
of God's promises

2 Corinthians 1:20

In this verse, as we noted in the previous chapter, the apostle affirms two things: first, all God's promises are in Christ; secondly, all God's promises in Christ are 'Yes' and 'Amen' in him. In the last chapter, we looked at what it means to say God's promises are in Christ. Now we come to this matter of what it means to say they are 'Yes' and 'Amen' in Christ.

The triumphant climax of a long-awaited fulfilment

The first promise God made to mankind was to Adam and Eve in the Garden of Eden. It was the promise that Christ would come to provide eternal salvation for all those who embrace him as Lord and Saviour. Christ did not come for many centuries after that promise was given, and there were many times that the promise of his coming looked as if it would never be fulfilled.

Adam and Eve must have wondered about its fulfilment. When Cain was born, Eve said, 'I have gotten a man from the Lord' (Gen. 4:1). That statement indicates that Eve thought her firstborn, Cain, was to be the fulfilment of the promise God had given her and Adam. But, far from being the fulfilment of the promise, Cain did not even embrace it, but was so hostile towards it that he actually murdered his own brother, Abel.

Adam and Eve suddenly found themselves left with only one son, the son who had rebelled against the promise. But God soon gave them another son, Seth, and the promise was secure.

Years passed, and the world became so wicked that it appeared that it would perish under the weight of its wickedness. Jonathan Edwards says of this period: 'Satan seems to have been in a dreadful rage just before the flood, and his rage then doubtless was, as it always has been, chiefly against the church of God to overthrow it ... and the church was reduced to so narrow limits, as to be confined to one family. There was no prospect of any thing else but of their totally swallowing up the church, and that in a very little time; and so wholly destroying that small root that had the blessing in it, whence the Redeemer was to proceed.'[1] But God preserved that 'small root' by keeping Noah and his family safe in the ark while the rest of the world perished in a great flood.

God later singled out the family of Abraham as the one through whom the promise of the Christ was to be fulfilled. There were many instances in which it seemed certain that the family of Abraham would be obliterated and, with it, the promise of the Messiah. But God preserved Abraham's family and his promise. He saw to it that Abraham's descendants were not destroyed by the Canaanites around them, even though there were cases where it appeared as if they would be (Gen. 35:1-5). When a severe famine threatened the existence of the chosen family, God had his Joseph there in Egypt to preserve them (Gen. 50:20).

After the family settled in Egypt under Joseph, they grew into a great nation. Edwards says of this time: 'This now was the third time that God's church was almost swallowed up and carried away with the wickedness of the world; once before the flood; the other time, before the calling of Abraham; and now, the third time, in Egypt. But yet God did not suffer his church to be quite overwhelmed: he still saved it, like the ark in the

flood, and as he saved Moses in the midst of the waters in an
ark of bulrushes, where he was in the utmost danger of being
swallowed up. The true religion was still kept up with some;
and God had still a people among them, even in this miserable,
corrupt, and dark time.'[2]

On and on we could go. During the time of the judges,
apostasy ran at floodtide in the nation of Israel, but God still
preserved his people and his promise.

Centuries later idolatry became so rampant among his
people that God sent them into captivity in Babylon for
seventy years. There it finally seemed that they would be
swallowed up by that culture and that all God planned and
purposed to do would come to nought. But God preserved his
people there, brought them back to their homeland and re-
established them as a nation.

Then came what we know as the 'inter-testamental period',
that long period of four hundred years of silence in which God
ceased to speak to his people. During that time, it appeared that
God himself had forgotten his promise, that he was no longer
interested in sustaining it or fulfilling it. But such was not the
case. The New Testament opens with God speaking to Mary,
Joseph, Elizabeth and Zacharias. His messages to them proved
his promise was not null and void. It was still in effect.
Elizabeth was to bear the forerunner of the Messiah, and Mary
was to bear the Messiah himself (Matt. 1; Luke 1).

Then one night outside the village of Bethlehem, shepherds
were startled and astounded by the appearance of an angel.
This angel delivered glorious news: 'Do not be afraid, for
behold, I bring you good tidings of great joy which will be to
all people. For there is born to you this day in the city of David
a Saviour, who is Christ the Lord' (Luke 2:10-11).

The long-awaited Messiah had finally come! When Christ
stepped into human history as a mere baby, it was as if he
shouted a resounding, 'Yes, the promise of God is fulfilled.'

It was as if he shouted a thunderous, 'Amen, it is true,' to the promise God had made. He was, then, the 'Yes' and the 'Amen' to God's promise that he would indeed come.

The inevitable deduction

The promise of Christ is, of course, God's greatest promise. It is, as we have noted, what Richard Sibbes refers to as the 'grand' promise. It is the hinge on which all the other promises turn.

This leads us to an inevitable deduction. If, in the birth of Jesus, God fulfilled the greatest of all his promises, we can rest assured that all his other promises are reliable as well. If he fulfilled the greatest, why should he not fulfil all the others? The coming of Christ is, therefore, in and of itself the single greatest guarantee of the reliability of all God's promises.

God has promised great good to each of his children. He has promised to walk with us during our time in this world and then to take us home to himself in a realm of unfathomable glory and splendour. But we are living in a world of scepticism and doubt, and, if we are not careful, that scepticism and doubt can 'rub off' onto us. It is possible to be a Christian while not being robust in faith or filled with joy.

What is the Christian to do to maintain a robust faith and an abounding joy? Dwell on the promises of God. And how may the Christian be wholly convinced of the certainty of God's promises? Look to the Lord Jesus Christ! He was, and is, against seemingly impossible odds, the fulfilment of God's greatest promise, and he is, therefore, the guarantee of the fulfilment of all the others.

When the nation of Israel was finally settled in the land of Canaan and they were able to look back on all their experiences, Joshua said, 'Not a word failed of any good thing which the Lord had spoken to the house of Israel. All came to pass' (Josh. 21:45; 23:14).

And when he dedicated the temple, King Solomon was able to say to the people: 'Blessed be the Lord, who has given rest to his people Israel, according to all that he promised. There has not failed one word of all his good promise, which he promised through his servant Moses' (1 Kings 8:56).

These men employed absolute language. They did not merely affirm that God had kept most of his promises, but rather that he had kept every single word of each one of his promises.

When God's people finally come to the end of their journey and look back on it all, they will certainly find themselves agreeing with Joshua and Solomon. Not one word of one promise failed. We can trust the God who sent Christ to do all he has promised.

Section II
Promises for setting off

The Christian is a pilgrim. The apostle Paul says, 'Our citizenship is in heaven, from which we also eagerly wait for the Saviour, the Lord Jesus Christ...' (Phil. 3:20). The apostle Peter referred to his readers as 'pilgrims' (1 Peter 1:1), and the author of Hebrews calls the Old Testament saints 'strangers and pilgrims on the earth' (Heb. 11:13).

An old hymn states the same truth in a rather quaint way:

This world is not my home,
I'm just a-passing through.
My treasures are laid up
Somewhere beyond the blue.

Every journey has three parts — a departure from one point, an arrival at another point and a traversing of the distance between those two points. The Christian's life can be divided into these same three categories. The Christian has a point of departure. He or she was not born a Christian but, along with everyone else, came into this world as a citizen of the kingdom of Satan, or, to use John Bunyan's term, a citizen of the City of Destruction.

How, then, did the Christian come to depart from that woeful citizenry? How did he get started on the road to eternal life? The answer is that he came to hear some good news, gloriously good news. The King of the kingdom of life and light has made promises to all the citizens of Satan's kingdom who will receive them.

This section looks at some of the promises that come to the sinner's ears when God plucks him from the City of Destruction and places his feet on the path of life.

6.
God's promise to save the believing sinner

Romans 10:1-13

The word 'saved' occurs frequently in the New Testament. It appears three times in this passage (vv. 1,9,13) and the word 'salvation' appears once (v. 10).

Everyone understands the meaning of the word 'saved' in its physical context. It means a person has been rescued, or delivered, from great danger. We might say he or she has been brought from a position of peril into a state of safety and well-being. The word means exactly the same in the spiritual realm.

Our grave danger

First, the Bible tells us we are all by nature in a state of extreme danger. This is due to the fact that we must all leave this world some day and stand before God.

To understand this state of danger, we must first understand that God is perfectly holy and righteous. The Bible unrelentingly stresses this truth. It ascribes holiness to each person of the Trinity. God the Father is holy (John 17:11). God the Son is holy (Mark 1:24). The Spirit of God is called the 'Holy Spirit' no less than ninety-one times in the Bible.

The apostle John flatly affirms the holiness of God in these words: 'This is the message which we have heard from him and declare to you, that God is light and in him is no darkness at all' (1 John 1:5).

We turn to the Old Testament and we find the seraphim around God's throne crying, 'Holy, holy, holy is the Lord of hosts…' (Isa. 6:3). We turn to the New Testament and there are four living creatures around the throne of God ceaselessly crying, 'Holy, holy, holy, Lord God Almighty…!' (Rev. 4:8).

But it is one thing to know God is holy, and something quite different to realize what it means. For one thing, God's holiness means he cannot tolerate sin or compromise with it. Most of us have never even begun to have any idea or understanding of the complete and utter revulsion God feels towards our sins. The Bible pictures it for us in a couple of very graphic ways. It tells us, for instance, that God 'burns' with indignation against our sins (Heb. 10:27; 12:29). It also tells us God loathes sin to the point of vomiting (Lev. 18:25-28; 20:22-23; Rev. 3:16).[1]

This inevitably leads to something else. If God so detests our sin here and now, we may be absolutely certain that he will not tolerate it in heaven. The apostle John writes of the heavenly city: 'But there shall by no means enter it anything that defiles, or causes an abomination or a lie…' (Rev. 21:27).

One poet expressed the teaching of John in these lines:

There is a city bright;
Closed are its gates to sin;
Nought that defileth,
Nought that defileth,
Can ever enter in.

If we are to understand the state of danger we are in, we must also understand that we are anything but righteous and holy. God demands a perfect righteousness of us, and we have absolutely none to offer.

Paul's letter to the Romans sets our true condition in a glaring light. Four words summarize it: depravity, enmity, inability and universality.

Depravity means no part of our existence is free from the taint of sin. Paul portrays our depravity by compiling several phrases from the Old Testament (Rom. 3:13-18). The finished product is a devastating statement on the nature of sin. Readily apparent in this statement are the various parts of the body: throat, tongue, lips, mouth, feet, eyes. What it amounts to is Paul affirming that no matter how we look at man, no matter whether we turn him this way or that, we can see the sin and the foulness in him.

Enmity means we are by nature in a state of hostility towards God (Rom. 8:7). We are not only unable to meet God's standard; we actually resent it.

Inability means sin has so damaged us that we do not understand or seek after God (Rom. 3:11). Sin has completely incapacitated us. The sinner's mind is blind to the truth of God (2 Cor. 4:4), his heart is alienated from God, so that he embraces 'things on the earth' (Col. 3:2), and his will is completely enslaved (John 5:40).

Universality means we all without exception have the depravity, enmity and inability described above. Is sin really universal? Look for the words 'none' and 'all' in the following verses, and you will have Paul's answer:

There is none righteous, no, not one;
There is none who understands;
There is none who seeks after God.
They have all gone out of the way;
They have together become unprofitable;
There is none who does good, no, not one

(Rom. 3:10-13).

So here is our dreadful and grave danger. God demands one hundred per cent righteousness of us before he will allow us to enter heaven, and we have absolutely no righteousness to offer.

Have you ever felt the weight of this dreadful dilemma? Does it seem no one will go to heaven? Does heaven seem hopelessly out of reach? Some would argue that God cannot possibly insist on perfect righteousness as the condition for getting into heaven because such a demand would make heaven a ghost town!

Gracious deliverance

With these things in mind, we come to this tenth chapter of Romans and the promise it contains. The first half of this chapter answers for us the great question of how we may stand clean and righteous before a holy God.

In theory, there are two ways to render to God this righteousness that he demands, but in reality there is only one. Theoretically, one way to meet God's righteous demands would be through 'law righteousness' or 'works righteousness'. Even though God did not give the moral law as a means of salvation, if anyone could perfectly keep that law he or she would be righteous in the eyes of God. This would require that this person should not even sin once in word, thought, or deed. If someone could do this, he would be righteous before God. This is what Paul means when he quotes Leviticus 18:5: 'The man who does those things shall live by them' (Rom. 10:5).

The whole problem, as we have seen, is that sin has such a grip on us that we cannot possibly keep the law of God. The Jews thought they could, and they worked very diligently at it, but all they succeeded in doing was to make themselves think they were righteous. They came nowhere near achieving the perfect righteousness that God demands (v. 3). 'Law righteousness', then, is a righteousness in theory only because it is impossible for sinful human beings to achieve.

Thank God, there is another kind of righteousness available to us. It is 'faith righteousness'. This is the righteousness we do not provide for ourselves. It is rather the righteousness provided for us by God himself. How did God provide this righteousness? Paul answers by saying, 'Christ is the end of the law for righteousness to everyone who believes' (v. 4).

How did God provide righteousness in and through Jesus Christ? First, the Lord Jesus Christ lived a life of perfect obedience to God. He is the only one who has ever had 'law righteousness'. He did not break the law of God even in one single point.

After living that perfect life, the Lord Jesus went to the cross and died. His death there was no ordinary death. It was rather a 'propitiation' (Rom. 3:25). That means Jesus satisfied the wrath of God against our sins by actually bearing the punishment for them.

So Christ provided by his life the righteousness we need and by his death paid for the sins that we have committed.

How do we get what Christ did to count for us? Here is the promise: 'If you confess with your mouth the Lord Jesus and believe in your heart that God has raised him from the dead, you will be saved' (Rom. 10:9). It is all by faith! Faith hears the good news about the righteousness Christ has provided by his life and the atonement he has provided by his death, and it wholeheartedly embraces this good news.

Faith is nothing less than totally resting on the finished work of the Lord Jesus Christ as the only means of meeting God's demands. It submits to and relies on the righteousness God has provided in him. It does not quarrel with, or find fault with, God's plan of salvation, but delights in it.

To help us grasp this point, Paul pictures faith speaking for itself. If I may put it this way, he has faith come to the pulpit and do the preaching about itself.

What does faith have to say about itself? What is the word of this preacher, faith? It is this: Jesus Christ has done everything necessary for us to be saved. It tells us there is no need to scour heaven to find someone to come down and provide the righteousness we need to get into heaven. Christ has already come down and provided it (v. 6). And he has already gone back into heaven to represent us before God (v. 7). The work of salvation is done!

Furthermore, faith declares that the word of salvation is near (v. 8). Every time the gospel message is preached, faith comes, as it were, to the sinner's ear and says, 'Salvation is not far away. It is here now in this message. Believe the word about Christ and receive his work as your only hope.'

The message of faith, then, is that we should rest ourselves entirely upon the work of Jesus Christ, and, having rested upon it, confess it openly (vv. 9-11).

It is very important that we realize confession goes hand in hand with faith. Some think they have saving faith if they merely believe in their hearts, that no open confession is necessary. Others think they can confess that they are following Jesus as Lord and not have to be committed to him in their hearts. Paul will have none of this. He says we must have both a believing confession and a confessing belief.

He who hears the message of salvation, rests upon it and openly confesses it is forgiven of his sins. He is saved. He does not have to fear standing before a holy God because he has been clothed in the perfect righteousness of the Lord Jesus Christ.

7.

God's promise to be the God and Father of those who believe

2 Corinthians 6:16 - 7:1

The promise of God to forgive all those who believe in Christ is astounding beyond words. If we had no other promise from God, we would be immeasurably blessed. But God has even gone beyond this. He has not only stooped low to pluck us out of the misery of our sins, but he has also reached so high as to lift us to a higher plane than we ever thought imaginable. This higher plane is laid out for us in Paul's second letter to the Corinthians.

The Christians in Corinth were called to the risky business of walking a high wire. On one hand, they were required by their Lord Jesus Christ to maintain contact with the world so that they could share his gospel with it. But on the other hand, they were required to maintain a distinct separation from the world.

In the verses before us, the apostle Paul was dealing with the danger of toppling off the high wire into compromise with their society and accommodation of it. This was no small temptation. The city of Corinth was not only thoroughly pagan, but militantly so. Corinthian culture put a lot of pressure on all who came into contact with it to throw convictions and principles to the wind and give themselves to the tide.

In his first letter to the Corinthians, the apostle had sounded the alarm about the importance of being separate from the world, but his warning had evidently been disregarded. Here he renews it under the imagery of being 'unequally yoked' (v. 14). His image of the yoke gives us insight into this whole matter of the Christian's relationship to the world. If we may carry the analogy a bit further, we may say it is all right to be in the same barn with an unbeliever, but not under the same yoke. A yoke implies unity of purpose and effort. The Christian must avoid those yokes that require two people to agree on what is most important in life and on what life's most important goals and priorities should be.

In warning the Corinthians about the peril of an unequal yoke, the apostle did something very unusual and striking. He ranged over his Old Testament Scriptures, selecting promises here and there, to create the cluster of promises we have here in verses 16-18.

As we look at these verses, we can see Paul doing primarily two things. First, he gives an explanation of who the Christian is. Then he gives an exhortation about how the Christian is to behave.

An explanation

We look first at his word of explanation (vv. 16-18). Perhaps the best way to explain the Christian is in this way: he is one who has not been left to go his own way but God himself is actively at work in his life.

It should not escape our notice that one of Paul's quotations from the Old Testament includes a verse in which God identifies himself as 'the Lord Almighty' (v. 18; 2 Sam. 7:14). This mighty God is the one who is at work in the life of each and every Christian.

Four times in these verses, God says, 'I will...' I try to be careful about saying 'I will'. There is a definiteness and a certitude there that I am not always able to deliver. I use terms like 'I want' and 'I hope', but the mighty God does not have to leave any room for failure. He simply says, 'I will'.

Now what has this mighty God done in the lives of believers? In this passage, Paul chooses to emphasize only a couple of things — reconciliation and adoption.

Reconciliation

Reconciliation is the theme of verse 16. There Paul quotes words that are found in Leviticus 26:12. The latter part of this quotation is also found in Jeremiah 32:38 and Ezekiel 37:27. What does the word 'reconciliation' mean? J. I. Packer answers: 'The general idea conveyed by the Greek root from which the relevant terms are formed is that of change or exchange, and the regular meaning which these terms bear both in secular Greek and in the Bible is that of a change of relations, an exchange of antagonism for amity, a turning of enmity into friendship. To reconcile means to bring together again persons who had previously fallen out; to replace alienation, hostility and opposition by a new relationship of favour, goodwill and peace; and so to transform the attitude of the persons reconciled towards each other and to set their subsequent mutual dealings on a wholly new footing.'[1]

When God talks, then, about dwelling with people and walking with them (as he does in the verses Paul quoted), we know reconciliation has taken place between him and those people. As difficult as it may be for modern men and women to accept, the truth of the matter is that we are not naturally in a state of peace with God. According to the Bible, we come into this world with a sinful human nature that is hostile towards God and opposed to his ways. The apostle Paul puts it bluntly in Romans 8:7: 'The carnal mind is enmity against God; for it is not subject to the law of God, nor indeed can be.'

Furthermore, the Bible tells us not only that we are by nature opposed to God, but he is also opposed to us. The Bible insists that God is holy, and his holiness means he cannot be ambivalent towards our sin. David recognized this and, in the light of it, says to God, 'For you are not a God who takes pleasure in wickedness, nor shall evil dwell with you' (Ps. 5:4).

But here in 2 Corinthians we find God suddenly speaking of dwelling with people and walking with them. He speaks of being their God and their being his people. What has taken place? The enmity has been put aside and now there is peace. These people and God are no longer at war with each other!

How did such a marvellous reconciliation come about? The apostle Paul answers that question in his letter to the Romans. There he says, 'For if when we were enemies we were reconciled to God through the death of his Son, much more, having been reconciled, we shall be saved by his life' (Rom. 5:10).

That phrase, 'through the death of his Son', tells us how sinful people can be reconciled to God so that he dwells with them and walks with them. It is only through the atoning death of the Lord Jesus Christ. There, on the cross, he bore in his own person the penalty of God against those who believe. Since Christ paid the penalty for sin, God's wrath against sin has been satisfied and there is, therefore, no more reason for him to be at war with us. The source of the enmity, our sin, is removed, and the way is cleared for us to be at peace with God.

It is very important that we realize that God himself is the one who did what was necessary for this reconciliation to take place. He is the one who sent the Lord Jesus Christ to die that reconciling death on the cross.

Adoption

The second thing that the mighty God does for his people can be summarized with the word 'adoption'. This truth is brought out by Paul's quotation of Ezekiel 20:34,41. Here Paul takes us to an even higher level. God has not only promised to reconcile his people through the death of Christ, but to exalt them to such a high position that he actually regards them as his own dear children. What a great gap is spanned by redemption — all the way from being enemies of God to being his own sons and daughters!

As we look at the Scriptures we find God promising many things to his people. His grand promise is, as we have noted, the Lord Jesus Christ himself and the salvation he came to provide. But there are also promises that relate to our trials and burdens in this life. These many promises are nothing less than a Father expressing his tender concern for his children and providing for their needs.

Much more could be said about God's promises of reconciliation and adoption. These are promises that have already been realized by all those who have come to God by faith in the substitutionary, atoning death of the Lord Jesus Christ. But those promises are still there for all those who have not yet received them. The plea of the Scriptures to all those who have not received these promises is this: 'Be reconciled to God' (2 Cor. 5:20).

An exhortation

But we must move now from Paul's word of explanation about who the Christian is to his word of exhortation.

Christians have been reconciled and adopted. They are no longer God's enemies, but rather his children! What wonderful blessings! What should our response be to such blessings? Paul has the answer ready for us. He says, 'Therefore, having these promises, beloved, let us cleanse ourselves from all filthiness of the flesh and spirit, perfecting holiness in the fear of God' (7:1).

In other words, Paul brings these blessings of reconciliation and adoption to bear on this matter that was troubling the Corinthians, namely, how to live in a godless society. The way for the Corinthians to stand firm in a culture that desired to press them into its mould was to remember how blessed they were!

Theologians have called God's plan to reconcile and adopt us 'the covenant of grace'. William Hendriksen defines the covenant of grace in this way: 'It is that arrangement between the Triune God and his people whereby God promises his friendship, hence full and free, to his people, upon the basis of the vicarious atonement of Christ, the Mediator of the covenant, and they, out of gratitude, promise to live for him.'[2]

God alone can do the saving. We cannot do it ourselves. But once we are saved, we can express our gratitude to him by living holy lives. When modern-day 'Corinthians' put the pressure on us to think the way they think and act the way they act, we must deliberately and ruthlessly call to mind the facts of our reconciliation and adoption. We must reflect long and hard on the truth that we were once God's enemies, but he took it upon himself to make peace with us at the dreadful cost of giving up his own Son. We must reflect long and hard on the fact that he has taken us to the high level of placing us in his own family. As we reflect on these promises that have already been fulfilled in us, we can say to our wicked age what Joseph said to Potiphar's wife: 'How then can I do this great wickedness, and sin against God?' (Gen. 39:9).

8.
God's promise to grant rest for the soul

Matthew 11:28-30

These beautiful and well-known words from the Lord Jesus give us yet another aspect of the beginning of the Christian's journey. He has his sins forgiven. He has been reconciled to God and adopted into his family. But, thank God, he also has been promised rest for his soul. Rest for the soul — what a pleasant and appealing thought! That means the mind is not tormented with uncertainty and doubts; the conscience is not tortured with feelings of guilt; the heart is not torn by competing drives and desires.

That is what Jesus promises: rest for the soul! It sounds marvellous, doesn't it? Do you have it? Can you say right now that your soul is at rest and peace? If not, are you aware of what you must do to make this peace and rest yours?

Consciousness of need

You must first be conscious of your great need for this rest. Notice that Jesus addresses his promise to those who 'labour and are heavy laden' (v. 28). There are two separate and distinct thoughts in that phrase. Labouring is different from being heavy laden. To labour is to put forth effort and toil. It is to be active. But to be heavy laden is a passive thing. It is to have a burden placed on one's back, then to have to endure that burden.

Are you conscious of labouring? Are you someone who has become aware that there is something dreadfully wrong in your life and you are frantically searching for the answer? Are you conscious of the fact that you must someday leave this life and stand before the eternal God who has the power to plunge you into eternal darkness and despair? Are you feverishly searching for a way to stand clean and guiltless before him on that day?

Martin Luther was one of those who laboured. He became conscious of the fact that he had to stand before God and give account of himself. Furthermore, he could see life steadily passing by and the Day of Judgement swiftly hastening towards him. The only thing Luther knew to do was to labour. He frantically tried to accumulate enough good works to make himself acceptable to God. Many today can identify with Luther. They are labouring for eternal life.

Perhaps you are conscious of being loaded down with a heavy burden. You know you are guilty before God, that you have broken his laws time without number, that you are deserving only of his wrath and condemnation. Each day you plod along carrying this heavy knowledge and you do not know what to do. Life seems to be intolerable and yet you are afraid to die.

What shall we say to those who are labouring and are heavy laden? If you find yourself in one of these categories, I have one word to say about you: 'Good!' Does that sound like a very harsh and unfeeling thing to say? Most would probably say it is. We tend to think it is a terrible thing for anyone to be struggling and labouring and to be carrying a heavy load. But when it comes to spiritual matters, it is good for people to be labouring and heavy laden because they, and they alone, can receive the rest that Jesus promises in these verses.

This feeling of struggling and being heavily burdened is what former generations of Christians referred to as conviction. We do not often hear that term these days but there can be no rest of soul for anyone until he passes through this stage of conviction. No one can be saved until he sees the need for salvation, and he will not see that need until he realizes the depth of his sins.

Let's suppose you have been made conscious of your great need and that you know all about this business of labouring and being heavy laden. What comes next? What do you have to do to find this rest that Jesus promises?

Coming to Christ

The answer is that you must come to Christ. Jesus says, 'Come to me, all you who labour and are heavy laden, and I will give you rest.'

But what does it mean to come to Christ? The Lord Jesus does not leave us in suspense, or to decide for ourselves what is involved here. He says it means to take his yoke upon us and to learn of him.

When Jesus referred to *the yoke*, everyone in his audience knew what he was talking about. The yoke was a device that was placed over the neck of an ox to allow it to pull a plough or a cart. That was a single yoke. A double yoke connected one ox with another to form a team.

In either case, the yoke represented submission to authority and servitude. When the yoke was placed on the ox it was to subject the animal to the owner's authority and to secure its service. So it is with anyone who comes to Christ. He ceases to be his own authority and he starts to live under the authority of Jesus. He stops serving himself and he starts serving the Lord.

How sorely we need to understand that coming to Christ involves submission and servitude! Multitudes assure themselves that it is possible to come to Christ for salvation without having the slightest interest in submitting to and serving him. But Jesus says it is impossible to have one (the coming) without the other (the yoke of service).

But that is not all. Coming to Christ not only means taking his yoke but *learning from him* (v. 29). In other words, the Lord was not content merely to say that we must submit to his authority. He went on to say specifically that we are to submit our minds to his teaching. Why did the Lord go on to include this? Could it be that we have more trouble submitting in this area of the mind than anywhere else?

Millions today are not willing to learn from Christ. They hear his teaching on some matter and they immediately want to dispute it and take issue with it. Sometimes they respond to biblical teachings by saying, 'That doesn't seem fair.' Or they might respond by saying, 'Times have changed. We surely can't be expected to believe such things now.'

When we take such words on our lips we are refusing to learn from Christ. We are refusing to walk under his yoke. The person who has truly come to Christ accepts the teachings of Christ. The Lord has some very definite things to say about man's sinfulness. He has some unvarnished teachings on God's wrath against our sin. He also, thank God, has some clear things to say about the salvation that he came to provide by his death on the cross. The man who comes to Christ accepts these teachings; he does not quarrel with them but simply listens, accepts and acts upon them.

Coming to Christ, then, is not the light, trivial thing we so often make it out to be. It is not just a matter of coming forward during an invitation, or of nodding general assent to a few propositions about Christ. It involves submission and servitude and this, in turn, means learning from Christ.

In the light of these things, can you say you have truly come to Christ? Are you walking under his yoke of submission and service? Are you hearing his teachings and accepting them?

Perhaps you think all of this is far too demanding. Jesus knew some would respond in that way, so he went on to say, 'My yoke is easy and my burden is light' (v. 30). Yes, coming to Jesus involves wearing a yoke. Yes, coming to Jesus means bearing a burden. But compared to the yoke and the burden of sin, the yoke and the burden of Christ are light indeed.

Christians have to smile when they hear unbelievers talk about how hard the Christian life is. What is hard is the life of sin. Sin wrecks the body and brings guilt and unhappiness in this life, then it destroys the person for ever in the life to come. Now that is hard! There is no rest in a life like that.

But there is rest in coming to Christ. There is rest in knowing our sins are forgiven. There is rest in knowing we have nothing to fear when we leave this life and stand before God at the judgement. There is rest in knowing that we have heaven for our home.

Section III
Promises for the journey

The person who receives God's promises of salvation is not suddenly whisked by God from this earth into heaven. He or she has, by the grace of God, departed from sin and destruction and started upon a journey in this earthly realm. That journey may be long, or it may be short, but this much the Christian will certainly find: the journey will be challenging and difficult.

What makes the journey so challenging? Christians have been left to journey upon this earth that they might 'proclaim the praises' of the God who 'called' them 'out of darkness into … marvellous light' (1 Peter 2:9). But the people of the world are still in darkness, and the Bible tells us that they love that darkness and are naturally antagonistic towards the light of God (John 3:19). The Christian is called, therefore, to make his journey through hostile territory.

If that were not enough, he also finds that there is such a thing as indwelling sin. Sin's power has been decisively defeated in his life, but it still conducts, as it were, a guerilla warfare against him. The Christian always finds himself wrestling with sin, often stumbling, continually lamenting his weakness and yearning for that glorious day when his salvation will finally be complete.

And, of course, Satan is ever busy to oppose the Christian in every way possible. So the Christian has that gloomy triad — the world, the flesh and the devil — to deal with in this life.

But the Christian also has something else — promises for the journey. God has given the believer promises to sustain, encourage, comfort and renew him as he journeys along life's treacherous pathway.

Life can also be a very challenging business for those who are not Christians and, in moments of despair, they are often known to lay claim to the promises given to the Christian to help him on his journey. But they are laying claim to what is not theirs. These are the salvation benefits purchased by Christ for his people.

Think of it in these terms. Suppose you and your family are sitting in your garden planning a summer holiday. With maps and travel brochures strewn everywhere you are excitedly discussing where you are going to go and what you are going to do. A neighbour suddenly walks up and says, 'Well, I think we should go here and there and do this and that.' What would your reaction be? After getting over the initial shock of this neighbour's audacity, you would probably say something like this: 'I'm sorry, but this is our holiday, and you really have nothing to do with it.'

When it comes to the promises of God, many people are like that audacious neighbour. They want to lay claim to something they really have no part of, and are not entitled to. We might say they want the benefits of knowing God without knowing God.

The fact is that most of God's promises are given only to his children and, contrary to popular opinion, all are not his children.

Essentially, God has made only two promises to those who are not his children. One is to bring them before his throne of judgement and there give them the result of their rejection of him, which is eternal destruction. The second is, as we have noted, to forgive those who truly cast themselves upon the Lord Jesus Christ.

The promises that follow, therefore, are given to those who have, by God's grace, acted upon the promises for setting off. These promises were given by God to help them on their journey.

How God's people should rejoice in these promises! Yes, the journey is difficult, but God has provided everything we need so we can join the psalmist in these glorious statements: 'The Lord is my shepherd; I shall not want' (Ps. 23:1). 'There is no want to those who fear him' (Ps. 34:9).

9.
The promise of a present Helper

John 14:16-18

The disciples of our Lord were crushed by the news that he was about to depart from this world and leave them behind. The Lord Jesus had a tender heart of concern for these men. What touched them touched him. He could not, therefore, ignore the grief and anguish in their hearts. How thankful we should be that our Lord has that same tender concern for all who are his disciples today!

It was this concern that compelled the Lord to give his disciples some comforting promises. One was that he would come again and take them to the Father's house (vv. 1-4). Another was that they would continue his works and would do even greater things than he had done (vv. 12-14).

In John 14:16-18 the Lord gives them yet another promise to console and encourage them. He speaks of a gift that he would secure for them. This gift was like no other the disciples had ever received: it was a person.

The Lord Jesus uses two names for this person. One is 'Helper' (v. 16). The other is 'Spirit of truth' (v. 17).

The Helper

The first of these names translates the Greek word *'paraclete'*, which literally means 'one called to be beside another'.

John Brown says, 'It was the custom, before the ancient tribunals, for the parties to appear in court, attended by one or more of their most powerful and influential friends, who were called *paracletes* — the Greek term — or advocates — the Latin term. They were not advocates in our sense of the term — fee'd counsel — they were persons who, prompted by affection, were disposed to stand by their friend; and persons, in whose knowledge, wisdom, and truth, the individual having the cause had confidence.'[1]

For more than three years the disciples had enjoyed a *paraclete* in the Lord Jesus Christ. He had come alongside them to stand by them as their friend. The fact that he was going to depart from them did not mean he was going to cease to be their *paraclete*. He would continue to represent them in the court of heaven. But he was going to cease to be their *paraclete* on earth, a place where the disciples would sorely need friendship and support as they encountered hostility and controversy. How could they ever face such things without the Lord Jesus Christ?

The Lord's words give the answer to this question. They would face these things with the aid of another helper. While the Lord Jesus was representing them in heaven, the Third Person of the Trinity, the Holy Spirit, would stand alongside them on earth, and he continues to do this work for all Christians today.

The Spirit of truth

Jesus also referred to the Holy Spirit as 'the Spirit of truth'. This tells us the Holy Spirit's work would have a particular connection with, or orientation towards, the truth of God.

We find a fuller statement from Jesus on this matter a little later in this very same discussion: 'However, when he, the

Spirit of truth, has come, he will guide you into all truth; for he will not speak on his own authority, but whatever he hears he will speak; and he will tell you things to come. He will glorify me, for he will take of what is mine and declare it to you. All things that the Father has are mine. Therefore I said that he will take of mine and declare it to you' (John 16:13-15).

These verses make it clear that the truth in which the Holy Spirit is vitally interested is that about the Lord Jesus Christ, or the truths of the gospel. He perfectly comprehends this truth, and he revealed it to the disciples and guided them into an understanding of it.

How sorely we need to understand this vital connection between the Holy Spirit and the truth about Jesus! To hear some people talk, one could easily get the impression that the Holy Spirit came into this world to 'do his own thing', and that his presence in the world means we have no further need of Christ.

Nothing could be further from the truth. The Holy Spirit came, not to call attention to himself, but to exalt and glorify Christ. He does this by opening our minds and our hearts to receive the truth about Christ. He is most pleased when we are most Christ-centred, and he is most grieved when we elevate his work above that of Christ.

How can you and I judge whether the Holy Spirit is really at work at a given time or in a given place? Some seem to think of him as some kind of force or emotional energy, and they conclude something is of the Spirit if there is a great deal of emotion or enthusiasm. If, for instance, people are moved and excited in a particular service, they do not hesitate to pronounce: 'The Holy Spirit was really in that service.' Or if a preacher is very dramatic and entertaining, they will quickly conclude that he has the anointing of the Spirit of God upon him. Such pronouncements blissfully ignore those episodes in Scripture in which people were filled with energy and excitement and were of the devil, as was the case with the prophets of Baal in 1 Kings 19.

The truth is that the Holy Spirit is not the only spirit in this world. There are many false spirits at work, and we are under the solemn obligation to test the spirits (1 John 4:1).

How shall we avoid being deceived by false spirits? We must keep in mind that the Holy Spirit is exactly what the Lord Jesus called him — the Spirit of truth — and we must judge whatever purports to be of him on this basis: does it correspond to the truth that he himself has revealed to us in Holy Scripture? And since Jesus Christ is the subject of Scripture, we can also ask whether this thing that purports to be of the Spirit is Christ-centred.

If we understand these things, we shall have a very different perspective on much of what goes on in our churches today. We shall judge the success of a service, not on whether we were emotionally moved, but on whether the truth of God was presented. And we shall understand that the man who stands in the pulpit does the very best he can do for us, not when he entertains us and makes us feel good, but when he faithfully proclaims to us the truth of God and lifts high the Lord Jesus Christ.

Oh, that the people of God would come to a fresh appreciation of the truth of God and the centrality of the Lord Jesus! The truth is what matters. Here these eleven disciples stood, in their fears and despondency, wondering how they would ever be able to face a hostile world without the Lord, and the promise he gave to sustain and comfort them was that another would come alongside them to support them in this hostile world, and the way he would support them was to hold before them the truth as it is in Jesus. That same Holy Spirit would make us strong in exactly the same way as he made them, namely, by constantly holding before us the truth of the gospel.

What great strength there is in knowing we have truth that can never be shaken or destroyed! Let the world laugh and rage, the Christian can say in the immortal words of Martin Luther:

Let goods and kindred go,
This mortal life also;
The body they may kill:
God's truth abideth still,
His kingdom is for ever.

It is this matter of truth that separates the Christian from all others. He became a Christian by virtue of the Spirit of truth working the truth about the Lord Jesus Christ into his heart and mind.

The preciousness of Christ's gift

What a privilege it is to have this truth and the Spirit who gives it! Not all have it. The Lord says the world 'cannot receive' the Spirit of truth (John 14:17).

'The world' refers to all those who are in their natural state, men and women who are apart from God and still in their sins. These, according to the Lord Jesus, 'cannot' receive the Spirit of truth. Left to themselves, they are utterly incapable of coming to the truth the Spirit has to offer. The apostle Paul puts it like this: 'The natural man does not receive the things of the Spirit of God, for they are foolishness to him; nor can he know them, because they are spiritually discerned' (1 Cor. 2:14).

Why is it that the natural man cannot receive the Spirit of truth? John Brown answers: 'While a man believes a lie, he cannot believe the truth, in direct opposition to that lie. It is not that it is impossible for a worldly man to become a spiritual man; but it is impossible for him, while a mere worldly man, to receive the Spirit. It is not that there is any physical impossibility in the case — that the man wants any of the faculties which are necessary to the apprehension of truth, or to a correspondent state of feeling — but that it is morally impossible for man to love falsehood and truth at the same time on the same subject. The teaching of the Spirit was never welcomed by a worldly man.'[2]

The natural man is blinded by his sin. He is unable to see his need of Christ. He cannot see himself hurtling towards a day of accounting in which he must stand before a holy God. He does not see his own sins for what they are. God himself must first enlighten the minds of sinners before they can receive the truth of the gospel.

The disciples to whom Jesus gave the promise of the Spirit were once in that dreadful position themselves. They were once blind to the truth, but they were no longer. Thank God for those four exceedingly precious words the Lord spoke to these men: 'But you know him' (John 14:17).

The Christian is the most blessed of all men. He has not only embraced the truth the Spirit of God teaches, but he has actually been indwelt by this same Spirit (v. 17) and will continue to be for ever (v. 16).

What a marvellous, consoling promise for these sorrowing disciples to hear! They were not going to be left to themselves. Another *paraclete*, the Spirit of truth, was going to come to them to indwell them and help them. All of this was to be procured for them by the finished work of the Lord Jesus Christ. What blessed men! And their blessings are the blessings of all who know the Lord Jesus as Saviour.

10.
The promise of perseverance

Philippians 1:6

The Christian is set on a journey at the time when the grace of God works faith and repentance into his or her heart. But it is possible to set out on a journey and not be able to finish it. And Satan is ever eager to assure many young Christians, and even some who have been Christians for a long time, that they will never be able to complete their journey.

The apostle Paul has an encouraging word for all who are troubled by this thought: 'He who has begun a good work in you will complete it until the day of Jesus Christ...'

Salvation — God's good work

Paul's words fall quite naturally and easily into three parts. For one thing, he calls salvation *a good work*. There can be no dispute or debate about that. If we saw someone saved from drowning, or rescued from a burning building, we would have no hesitation in saying a good work had been done.

Good as such things are, they pale in comparison to what has been done for the Christian. The believer has been delivered from something far worse than drowning or perishing in a fire. He has been delivered from the most dreadful fate imaginable, the fate the Bible refers to as 'everlasting destruction from the presence of the Lord' (2 Thess. 1:9).

Another thing Paul emphasizes is that salvation is *God's work*. The biblical authors never tired of stressing the truth that salvation is entirely due to the grace of God.

All we have to do to understand this is to go back to the imagery of the drowning man. How does he get rescued? Does he first swim to the shore, fetch the lifeguard, go back into the water and carry on drowning? How ridiculous! The drowning man is drowning because he is unable to do anything to help himself. He does nothing to fetch the lifeguard. The lifeguard plunges into the water, swims to where the drowning man is and pulls him out. And all the credit for the rescue of the drowning man goes to the lifeguard. No one gives any credit to the drowning man.

If the lifeguard throws the drowning man a rope, the man merely grasps it. He does not consider his seizing the rope to be anything worthy of praise. Not at all. All the praise goes to the lifeguard who threw him the rope.

In like manner, the sinner is perishing, and it is God who, in the form of his Son, plunged into the lake and pulled him out. Or, to put it another way, it is God who has thrown him the rope of salvation, and the sinner grasps it with the hand of faith. But he does not consider his receiving salvation to be worthy of any praise or credit. All the praise and all the glory for the salvation of the sinner go to God.

God is the one who chose us in Christ before the foundation of the world. God is the one who sent Christ to purchase our salvation. God is the one who gave the Holy Spirit to work in our hearts and bring us to faith. Salvation is God's work.

Salvation — an ongoing, sure work

The third element in Paul's words goes directly to this matter of whether we shall be able to complete the journey. Paul says not only that this good work of salvation is God's work, but also that it is *a sure work*. God starts it, and he will see it through.

In other words, God does not say to the sinner, 'I will start the work of salvation, but then it will be up to you to keep it.' If that were the case, salvation would be partly God's work and partly ours. But salvation is all God's work.

Salvation consists of three elements. The first is *justification*. This is the aspect in which God, on the basis of the atoning work of the Lord Jesus Christ, declares the sinner to be guiltless.

The final stage is *glorification*. That is the end of salvation. At that point God finally completes the process and we stand faultless before the throne of his glory (Jude 24).

The part that comes between justification and glorification is *sanctification*. That is the stage in which God steadily works in those whom he has justified to wean them away from sin and to cause them to grow in grace.

The important thing for us to see is this: if salvation is God's work, each part of the process is his work. We cannot say, therefore, that God simply starts the work and leaves us to finish it. It would no longer be his gracious work if that were the case.

The Bible affirms in several places that God not only saves us from sin, but also keeps us. Jesus emphasized the keeping power of God in these much-loved words: 'My sheep hear my voice, and I know them, and they follow me. And I give them eternal life, and they shall never perish; neither shall anyone snatch them out of my hand. My Father, who has given them to me, is greater than all; and no one is able to snatch them out of my Father's hand' (John 10:27-29).

That keeping power of God assures that those who have been saved will never lose their salvation. They will indeed complete the journey.

But we must hasten on to note how God goes about this keeping work. Some have mishandled and mangled this doctrine. They argue that if someone has been saved, he can live any way he wants and still go to heaven when he dies.

This teaching has in recent years become enshrined in what is known as the 'carnal Christian' theory. This teaching insists that there are not only two categories of people — the saved and the lost — but three. The third group consists of those who have been saved, but live like the lost. Now it is true, of course, that Christians can and do act carnally from time to time, but that differs from the 'carnal Christian' teaching, which asserts that a person can be a Christian and yet live continually in sin.

Words from the apostle Peter show the flaw of the 'carnal Christian' teaching and also cast light on how God keeps the saint. He says Christians are 'kept by the power of God through faith for salvation ready to be revealed in the last time' (1 Peter 1:5).

The point that is so often missed about God's keeping of the saved is that he keeps them in a very definite and distinct way, and that is *through their faith*. In other words, a person who has truly been saved is going to continue in faith. He or she is going to continue believing in Christ, confessing Christ, obeying Christ, serving Christ, loving Christ and worshipping Christ. That is a far cry from living continually in sin!

God preserves his people, then, by stirring them up to persevere in the faith. Several texts of Scripture explicitly affirm that God's people will continue in the faith.

Jesus himself said: 'If you abide in my word, you are my disciples indeed' (John 8:31).

The apostle Paul says we have been reconciled to God if we 'continue in the faith' (Col. 1:21-23).

The author of Hebrews affirms that we indeed belong to the Lord's 'house' if we 'hold fast the confidence and the rejoicing of the hope firm to the end' (Heb. 3:6).

A little later the same author adds: 'For we have become partakers of Christ if we hold the beginning of our confidence steadfast to the end...' (Heb. 3:14).

It is, of course, very obvious that many do make professions of faith only to fall away. Charles Spurgeon observed that people 'jump into their religion as men do into their morning bath, and then jump out again just as quickly, converted by the dozen, and unconverted one by one till the dozen has melted away.'[1]

But let us make sure we understand that what such people fall away from is not salvation but from the outward profession of it. Those who are truly saved will not fall away, but will be kept by God continually stirring them to faith.

The apostle John saw people fall away even as we do today, and he explained it in these terms: 'They went out from us, but they were not of us; for if they had been of us, they would have continued with us; but they went out that they might be made manifest, that none of them were of us' (1 John 2:19).

The true Christian will fall into sin from time to time. The true Christian will backslide. But the true Christian will never lose his salvation. As has often been observed, the believer, like a man on a shipboard, may fall on the deck, but he will never fall overboard.

The true Christian has been set to travelling by the grace of God, and, by the grace of God, he or she will travel all the way home.

11.
The promise of a secure word

Isaiah 40:6-8

The people to whom Isaiah addressed the last chapters of his prophecy (Isa. 40-66) were in great need of comfort. They had been torn away from everything they held near and dear and were forced to endure captivity in the strange land of Babylon. Year after weary year dragged by as they chafed under the yoke of their captors. Isaiah was not among these captives — indeed, he lived many years before the captivity took place — but his prophecy contains a message designed to bring them the comfort they so desperately needed.

In the opening verses of this fortieth chapter, Isaiah represents himself as one who has heard some glorious news regarding the future of his nation. He first hears God himself charge a prophet to announce to the city of Jerusalem that its time of trouble is about to come to an end (vv. 1-2). That prophet sees God coming into the midst of the people to lead them out of Babylon back to Jerusalem and immediately begins to cry out that God is about to return to Jerusalem and the way must be prepared for him (vv. 3-5).

Isaiah then hears God speak to the prophet again. This time God says, 'Cry out!' And immediately the prophet wants to know what he should cry. God answers his question by contrasting the temporal nature of man in all his glory with the lasting Word of God (vv. 6-8).

The grand deliverance announced in these verses was not completely fulfilled by the Jews' return to their land. There was a far greater deliverance on the horizon that was to be accomplished by the coming Messiah. It is clear from Isaiah's prophecy, and particularly from chapters 40-66, that he definitely had this greater deliverance in view. There is, therefore, something of an 'intertwining' in these chapters. The deliverance of the Jews from Babylon and the deliverance from sin through the Messiah are so amazingly similar that Isaiah could not help but glance from one to the other. And the language he used of the former was appropriate for the latter.

Therefore, just as there was a herald, or forerunner, sent to announce the coming of God to the captives in Babylon to conduct them back to Jerusalem and to tell them of the need to prepare his way; so John the Baptist was sent to announce the coming of the Messiah and to proclaim the need for each heart to prepare to receive him (Matt. 3:1-3). And just as the return of the captives would reveal the glory of the Lord, so the glory of the Lord would be revealed, in a far greater way, in the coming of the Messiah to deliver his people from their sins.

We may safely assume that Isaiah 40-66 became a source of great consolation and hope to the captives. When things looked utterly bleak and dismal, the captives could read the words of Isaiah and be cheered and comforted.

A problem

But there was a problem. The words of Isaiah were not the only words sounding in the ears of these captives. We can visualize the situation. Here is one of the captives who vents his frustration and doubt. He says he doubts that they will ever get back to their own land, that they are all going to perish in Babylon, and they might as well accept it. No sooner are the

words out of his mouth than one of his fellow captives reminds
him of Isaiah's message. This second captive says to the first,
'Don't give up hope. Remember what Isaiah said. We are
definitely going to be restored to our own land.'

But before the second captive finishes speaking, yet an-
other message sounds. A Babylonian official barks, 'You
Jews might as well forget your homeland and your precious
Isaiah. You aren't going anywhere!'

Or perhaps the Babylonians conducted regular 'captivity
seminars' in which they chided the captives for believing they
would ever be released and urged them to get used to Babylon.
Does this seem far-fetched? Read the prophecy of Daniel.
There you will find the Babylonians pressuring Daniel and his
three friends to forget the idea of a future Jewish state and
become Babylonian in their thinking and doing.

In their captivity, then, the captives had to decide which
word they were going to believe. Would they believe the word
of hope given by their God through one of their prophets? Or
would they believe the word of despair uttered by those who
did not know their God and who despised their faith?

Does this all sound familiar? It should. Christians today
find themselves in the very same situation. We too live in a day
of competing voices. On one hand, we have in Scripture that
which purports to be the Word of our God (2 Tim. 3:16). On
the other hand, we have an abundance of modern-day
Babylonians who are eager to assure us that we have been
duped, that our word from God is nothing more than the
speculations and imaginations of men who were as deluded as
we are.

What makes this such a tough dilemma is the attractiveness
and winsomeness of these 'Babylonians'. These are not the
kind of people who are easily dismissed or despised. They do
not drool on themselves or wipe their mouths with their
sleeves. They live in nice houses, wear nice clothes and drive

nice cars. They talk learnedly and with great self-assurance and poise. They are educated, articulate and sophisticated.

Who are these 'Babylonians'? They are the glamorous actors and actresses who easily move us to laughter or tears when we turn on the TV. They are the professors, the journalists, the analysts, the lobbyists, the talk-show guests and the politicians who incessantly and constantly lecture us on morals and ethics. But they are also the people we work with and spend our leisure with. They include our neighbours and relatives. The modern-day Babylonians are simply those who tell us not to believe the Word of God, who offer their own message to compete with the message we have received from God.

Sometimes their challenge to our belief in the Word of God comes clothed in the garb of intellectual superiority, and we are told that no thinking person can possibly hold to such outdated concepts as we find in the Bible. Sometimes their challenge comes to us in the garb of sweet innocence: 'You can go to church next Sunday. Let's go boating today.' But whether it comes in sophistication or simplicity the message of the Babylonians is always the same: 'Don't believe God.'

What were the captives to do when the pressure was really on? Were they to blindly accept the message served up by the Babylonian culture? Or were they to try to arrive at some sort of synthesis that would allow them to believe both the Babylonian message and the message of God?

The answer

Isaiah gave them the answer. He knew they would be facing this dilemma of competing messages in their new environment. So in the midst of his promises about their certain return to their homeland, he included a promise about the reliability of the Word of God: 'The grass withers, the flower fades, but the word of our God stands for ever' (v. 8)

The other promises contained in Isaiah's prophecy were glorious. But they all hinged on the promise of God's reliable Word. What does it matter how glorious a promise is if it cannot be trusted? God's Word can be trusted! That is what this promise tells us and, in so doing, it opens the way for us to enjoy the glory of all the other promises. Here we have, as it were, the key to the room where all the other keys are kept.

There is a great contrast here between what withers and fades and what stands for ever. What was destined to wither and fade? The Babylonian culture. The Babylonians in general were like the grass that withers, and the most appealing and attractive among them were like the beautiful flowers that fade. But whether we want to talk about grass or flowers, the result is the same: each withers and fades. So it is with mankind. Take the common, ordinary man or the calm, cool sophisticate; the result is still the same: each dies.

The message of the Babylonians was, then, the message of mere men. Yes, they would be very attractive and very persuasive, but they were just flesh — pretty flesh, cultured flesh, sophisticated flesh, yes, but still flesh! And flesh, no matter how attractively it may package itself, withers and fades away. And when the Babylonians withered and faded, their message would perish with them. Perishing men, if they preach only their own times and their own culture, preach a perishing message.

It is different with the message of God. Because God himself is eternal, his message is eternal. It will never fall to the ground but will always stand steadfast and firm.

The very fact that the people to whom Isaiah's prophecy was addressed were experiencing this terrible captivity was in and of itself sufficient proof of the steadfastness of God's Word. God had warned them before they settled in the land that sinful living would cause him to send them into captivity.

And as they ignored his warning and slipped increasingly into sin, he sent prophet after prophet to tell them this captivity was coming as God's judgement upon them. They refused to listen and continued in their sins, and God's Word proved to be true.

And the message of God about the return of the captives to their homeland also proved true. The proud Babylonians thought their empire was invincibly secure, but Cyrus, King of Persia, invaded the city of Babylon through open gates and overthrew it. A little later he issued a decree that allowed the Jews to go back to rebuild their nation. Babylon seemed secure, but God's Word was more secure. The Babylonian message to the captives fell to the ground, but God's Word stood.

And while we are on this point, that greater fulfilment on which Isaiah also had his eye also came to pass. One glad day the forerunner, John the Baptist, burst on the scene with his thundering message to prepare the way of the Lord. And the promised Messiah came, lived in perfect obedience to God's law and went to Calvary's cross to effect that glorious redemption Isaiah foresaw.

He has now given to all those who receive his redemption these promises to sustain us on our journey through life, and he has assured us that when our travelling is over he will receive us unto himself in realms of glory. The Babylonians of our day are quick to assure us that we have been taken in, that there is nothing to these promises. But we have the answer to their scepticism. It is this: if God were going to break a promise, it would have been the one that required him to send his Son to a shameful, agonizing death on the cross. The fact that he has kept that promise, at such a cost, gives us ironclad certainty that he will keep all the rest. We can, therefore, say a triumphant 'Amen!' to Paul's words: 'He who did not spare his own Son, but delivered him up for us all, how shall he not with him also freely give us all things?' (Rom. 8:32).

What are we to do when we too find ourselves under intense pressure? What are we to do in the face of competing messages? Are we to jettison our belief in the Word of God and swallow what our culture dishes out? Or are we to construct some sort of synthesis that will allow us to believe both messages?

The answer is the same for us as it was for the captives in Babylon. We have a reliable Word from God and we must believe it. This does not mean we can have nothing at all to do with our culture. We can listen to our culture when it does not contradict the truth of God. But when it does contradict the truth of God, we must listen to God.

In other words, the two messages that sound in our ears — the message to reject God's Word and the message to accept God's Word — are not equal messages. The former is the perishing message of perishing men, while the latter is the eternal message of the eternal God. Isaiah cries to us from his distant day not to exalt the word that falls over the Word that stands. He would have us say with John Newton:

My God has promised good to me,
His word my hope secures;
He will my shield and portion be
As long as life endures.

A secure word — that is what we have in the Word of God! Let the modern Babylonians deride and scoff! The Word of our God is going to stand! Has he given us promises? We can take them to the bank! Has he given us commands? We had better obey them! Not one jot or tittle of God's Word is going to fail. Study it. Meditate on it. Believe it. Live it. You will never regret trusting the Word that stands rather than those that fall and fade.

12.
God's promise of guidance

Proverbs 3:5-6

Proverbs is the book of paths. The words 'path' and 'way' occur at least thirty-three times in just the first five chapters of this book. And there are also several references to path-related words such as 'steps', 'foot', 'travel' and 'stumble'.

According to Proverbs, we are all involved in the business of pathfinding and pathwalking. That may sound simple enough, but in fact it is far from simple.

Pathfinding is hard. Life sets so many different paths before us that it can be hard to know which one to take. There are the major-decision type of paths that stretch out before us. Whom shall I marry? What kind of career am I going to pursue? Where am I going to get my education?

Then there are the moral-issue type of paths that confront us. Solomon, the author of Proverbs, does not take long to get to those. He talks about those who leave 'the paths of uprightness to walk in the ways of darkness' (Prov. 2:13).

Every single day of our lives we are confronted with these moral paths and we must make decisions. Sometimes we know what the right path is, but there are many times when the waymarkers are all down and the map lines seem to be smudged.

And then there is the question of *pathwalking*. Just finding the right path does not mean it will be an easy path to travel.

The right paths seem to have plenty of precipitous turns that cause us to lurch one way or the other and no shortage of bumps to jar and jolt us. We can marry the right person and still have tension in the home. We can choose what is morally right and still be ridiculed and scorned. Anyone who thinks seriously about the twin tasks of pathfinding and pathwalking soon feels like crying, 'Help!'

Proverbs 3 brings good news for all those who feel they are no match for pathfinding and pathwalking: help is available! We have here in this book of paths a promise that God will provide help.

There has been some debate on the exact nature of the help God offers to provide. Some versions translate the last phrase of verse 6 in this way: 'He shall direct your paths.' Others translate it: 'He will smooth your paths.' Which of these two translations should we adopt? I am willing to leave the technical experts to wrangle over that question. As one who has frequently felt himself overmatched and overwhelmed with both pathfinding and pathwalking, I am going to refuse to choose between them and simply embrace both options. Yes, I believe God can both direct me in the finding of the right paths and he can smooth those paths for me as I walk them.

The sufficiency of God

The proper place for us to begin an analysis of this promise, then, is with the sufficiency of God for pathfinding and pathwalking. We are not sufficient for those things, but he is.

What does it take to choose the proper paths? Wisdom. What does it take to face the challenges and difficulties of the paths we choose? Strength. The Lord has both in abundant supply!

If you need proof of *the wisdom of God*, all you have to do is look at the natural order. Where did all this complexity and beauty come from? Solomon says, 'The Lord by wisdom founded the earth; by understanding he established the heavens...' (v. 19). If God is capable of putting all the natural order together, we should never doubt that he has the wisdom to help us find the paths we should take.

On top of that is *the Lord's strength*. Solomon also covers that: 'Many are the plans in a man's heart, but it is the Lord's purpose that prevails' (Prov. 19:21, NIV). Later he adds: 'There is no wisdom, no insight, no plan that can succeed against the Lord' (Prov. 21:30, NIV).

Solomon was not the only one to point out the Lord's wisdom and power. Wherever we turn in the Bible, we find its authors emphasizing these attributes of God. Take Isaiah, for instance. He was given a preview of a dark time that was to come upon the people of his nation. The people had gone badly astray and chosen the paths of wickedness. As we have already noted, it can be very hard to walk the right paths, but it is even harder to walk the paths of evil. Isaiah's people were about to find out how hard those paths can be. They were about to be carried away captive into Babylon, and there they would find themselves crying out to God for strength to walk where their chosen path had led.

Isaiah was given a word that would prove inestimably precious in those days when even the strongest of men would feel the need for strength:

Have you not known?
Have you not heard?
The everlasting God, the Lord,
The Creator of the ends of the earth,
Neither faints nor is weary.
There is no searching of his understanding.

He gives power to the weak,
And to those who have no might he increases strength
(Isa. 40:28-29).

The channel through which God's sufficiency flows to us

The fact that God has enough wisdom and power to help us
with finding and walking the right paths is not enough. We
need to know how to bring his wisdom and power to bear upon
our lives. The promise also deals with that. It gives us the
channel through which God's sufficiency flows to us.

Two ingredients form the compound from which this
channel is made: trusting and acknowledging God. Solomon
says we are to trust the Lord with all our hearts and to
acknowledge him in all our ways.

Trusting God

What does it mean to trust God? We must be careful here.
Many assume it means merely to believe that God will do
anything they want done, but that amounts to nothing more
than what the world calls 'positive thinking'. Trusting God is
entirely different. It means taking him at his word.

In other words, faith is not just believing *in* God but
believing *God*. Matthew Poole says to trust God means to
'wholly and securely rely upon God's promises and providence for help and relief in all thine affairs and dangers'.[1]

Has God promised to help us with finding the right path and
with walking in it? Then we must depend on him to do so! He
has demonstrated his faithfulness to his promises time after
time, and we can rest assured that he will be faithful to this one
as well.

Trusting God sounds easy, but there is more to it than meets
the eye. Solomon tells us we must make sure our trust is

wholehearted, or entire. He says we are to trust God with 'all' our hearts. There is to be no half-hearted trust of a totally sufficient God! With that little word 'all', Solomon forces us to grapple with one of our most common and most crippling tendencies — the tendency to have a divided heart. What is a divided heart? It is a heart that partially trusts God and partially trusts something else. A Christian who reads his Bible and his horoscope could be an example of one who has a divided heart.

Solomon amplifies the meaning of trusting God with all our hearts by adding the phrase: 'And lean not on your own understanding.' Some have taken this to mean that Solomon was anti-intellectual, that he is saying that God does not intend us to use the brains he has given us. However, if only we keep the context clearly in mind, we shall have no trouble under-standing what Solomon means. He goes on to say that we are not to lean on our own understanding immediately after saying we are to trust in God. And trusting God means relying on what God has said. When God has spoken on a matter, we are not to lean on our own understanding. In other words, we are not to pit our own ideas against the Word of God. When God tells us something we are not to sit in judgement on it, or to dispute it, but to bow before it.

It is necessary for us to be reminded of this because there is so much in the Word of God that baffles and confounds us. The Lord's thoughts are not our thoughts and his ways are not our ways (Isa. 55:8-9).

Acknowledging God

After saying we are to trust God, Solomon goes on to say we are to acknowledge him. This means to confess our depend-ence upon him for guidance and strength. Note once again this must be entire. We must acknowledge him in *all* our ways.

Right here is where so many of us go astray. We want to acknowledge our need for God when the going gets rough, but the Lord wants us to acknowledge him every single day, in all our circumstances and in all our plans and undertakings. He wants us to ask him for guidance even when our circumstances seem clear and we think we know what to do, and even when we do not feel the need for any more strength than our own. The Lord would have us say with Annie S. Hawks:

> I need Thee every hour,
> Most gracious Lord;
> No tender voice like thine
> Can peace afford...
>
> I need thee every hour;
> Teach me thy will;
> And thy rich promises
> In me fulfil.

What is the outcome of acknowledging God in all our ways? Charles Bridges says, 'No step well prayed over will bring ultimate regret. Though the promise will not rend us infallible; our very error will be overruled for deeper humiliation and self-knowledge; and thus even this mysterious direction will in the end be gratefully acknowledged, "He led me forth in the right way"' (Ps. 107:7).[2]

The example of Christ

The Lord Jesus Christ is the supreme example of trusting God and acknowledging him in all our ways. He came to this world with a definite path laid out before him, a path that required him to endure much hardship and suffering and finally die an agonizing death on a Roman cross. As Jesus walked this path, he demonstrated complete trust in the Father. He manifested this trust time after time during his public ministry. On one occasion he said, 'I do not seek my own will but the will of the Father who sent me' (John 5:30). On another occasion he said, 'The Father has not left me alone, for I always do those things that please him' (John 8:29).

As the Lord Jesus demonstrated utter reliance upon the Father, he received strength for the path he had to walk. He received strength when he was tempted by Satan in the wilderness. He received strength to endure the hostility and hatred of the religious leaders. He received strength in the Garden of Gethsemane.

Because the Lord Jesus could say of the Father, 'I will put my trust in him' (Heb. 2:13), he was given the strength to become the 'author' of our salvation (Heb. 2:10). If the author of our salvation found strength through trusting the Father, how much more can those who follow him find strength for living through trusting the Father!

Are the tasks of pathfinding and pathwalking too much for you? Are you befuddled and bewildered by the number of paths? Are you despondent over the difficulty of the paths you have chosen? Latch on to this promise. There is a totally sufficient God who is able and willing to pour his sufficiency into our lives if we will trust and acknowledge him. We may not be able to detect God's guidance at the moment we are choosing a path and we may not be conscious of his strength while we are walking it, but his wisdom and strength will be with us. He did not promise that we would always be able to detect his wisdom and feel his strength. But he did promise to supply them. Trust him to do so and, at the end of life, you will see his wisdom and strength were there even when they did not appear to be.

13.
The promise of answered prayer

Matthew 7:7-8; 18:18-19; 21:21-22; Mark 11:22-24; John
14:13-14; 15:7; 16:23; James 5:13-15; 1 John 3:22; 5:14-15

Few promises are repeated more frequently in Scripture than
God's promise to answer the prayers of his people. This is
stated in varying ways in the scriptures listed at the head of this
chapter. It is also safe to say there are few promises that have
been more troubling to the children of God.

A sharp dilemma

Why should this promise be so troubling? In short, simply
because so often it seems not to be true. How many have asked
God for something only to not receive it?

Satan is, of course, not at a loss to explain such instances.
He quickly whispers in the Christian's ear: 'God's promise
seems not to be true because it isn't true.' From there he
hastens to assure us that Christianity is nothing but a farce that
has been foisted upon naïve, credulous people.

Christians have been hard-pressed to explain how the
promise can seem so straightforward and simple — 'Ask and
you will receive' — and at the same time for there to be so
many examples of asking and not receiving.

Perhaps the most popular way around this dilemma is to
locate the problem in our faith. Those who hold this view
assure us that the fault is not with God, who, they say, is indeed

ready to answer each and every request we make, but rather with ourselves. We ask God for something, but down deep inside we do not really believe we are going to receive it, and we do not receive it.

As far as these people are concerned, faith is a mere matter of positive thinking, and the key to getting what we want is to ask God for something, and then simply assume that it will be ours. We are told, in fact, that we should never even pray about the matter again, for that would be clear evidence of a lack of faith. We are simply to 'name it and claim it' and it will be ours.

The problem is that there are great numbers of people who have asked God for something and truly believed they would receive it, only to find that their request was not granted. Often the faith of these people seems to have been very strong indeed.

Martyn Lloyd-Jones cites the case of the well-known preacher, Andrew Murray, who was planning a preaching tour when his nephew fell ill. The preacher and his nephew prayed for healing and, assuming faith is the same thing as positive thinking, went on the preaching tour just as if the boy had been healed. Three weeks later the boy died.[1] Here we have people whose faith was beyond dispute asking God for something and not receiving it.

Because of many such experiences, some have all but given up on God's promises to answer prayer. What shall we say to this dilemma?

There are only two options available: we can say either that the promise of God is false, or that it does not mean what many have taken it to mean.

Resolving the dilemma

One of the keys to resolving this dilemma is to remember a couple of rules of scriptural interpretation:

1. We must pay careful attention to the context, that is, to the verses preceding and following the passage in question.

2. We must always seek to gather up all that Scripture says on a given subject and draw our conclusions on that basis, rather than on only one or two verses on the subject, and we are to interpret Scriptures that are less clear by those that are more clear.

When we apply these rules to the prayer promises in Scripture we find they do not give us the 'blank cheque' they so often are interpreted as giving. The context in which many of the promises are found exercises an element of control, or, in other words, a limit placed upon each one.

The limit imposed by a wise Father

Take Jesus' words in Matthew 7:7-8. They seem to offer a blank cheque: 'Ask, and it will be given to you...' What could be clearer? So we ask, and nothing happens. Has the promise failed? Hardly! When we look at the verses that both precede and follow this promise, we cannot help but notice how frequently the Lord Jesus makes reference to the Father in heaven (Matt. 5:45; 6:1,4,6,8,9,14,15,18,26,32; 7:11). The phrase, 'Ask, and it will be given to you...', is set, then, in the context of God as Father.

If God is our Father, that means we are his children. And what is true of children? Do they always know what is best for them? No. Do they always ask their parents for wise things? No. Do they not often desire to possess things that would prove to be harmful to them? Yes. Are they not limited in understanding? Yes. It is a very foolish parent who gives his child everything he asks for.

We all know this and accept it in the area of parenting, but we forget it when it comes to the spiritual realm. God is the

Father; we are the children. As children we often ask for things that are unwise and even harmful, but just as parents have the best interests of their children at heart in refusing to grant them their requests, so God the Father has the best interests of his children at heart at all times. He may not, therefore, give us everything we ask for, but he does give 'good things' to his children (Matt. 7:11).

I suggest, therefore, that the prayer promises of Scripture must always be interpreted with the wise prerogatives of our heavenly Father firmly in mind.

The limit imposed by the name of Christ

Other examples of the context exercising an element of control over the prayer promises are found in those that say God will grant our requests if we ask in the name of Christ (John 14:13-14; 16:23). Praying in the name of Jesus means we recognize what we noticed at the outset — that is, that all God's promised blessings come to us only through Christ. We have no standing before God, or any right to anything from his hand, apart from Christ.

But does this mean we may be assured of receiving whatever we request as long as we remember to tack on the words: 'in Jesus name'? To pray in the name of Jesus means we must pray in a manner consistent with who he is and what he stands for. Before presenting any petitions to God, then, we must ask ourselves, 'Can these petitions honestly be made in the name of Jesus? Are they honouring to him?'

When we truly test our petitions in this way, we shall be able to weed out a lot of requests that are selfish in nature, and we shall be able to proceed in confidence. William Hendriksen says of the prayer offered in Jesus' name: 'It is not difficult to see that such a prayer will *always* and *most certainly* be answered, for the one who utters it does not ever want anything that Christ does not want!'[2] (italics his).

The limit imposed by abiding in him

With one of the prayer promises, the Lord Jesus places upon our asking the condition that we must be abiding in him and his words in us (John 15:7). Our praying must, then, be informed by a walk of fellowship with him and by the clear teachings of his Word.

The limit imposed by other Scriptures

Not only do we find the context of prayer promises giving us an element of control; we also find the same thing when we compare the prayer promises with other passages of Scripture.

Those who have the 'blank cheque' mentality overlook those passages that tell us God does not even hear some of our prayers at all, let alone answer them. The psalmist says, 'If I regard iniquity in my heart, the Lord will not hear' (Ps. 66:18).

We find the same truth stated in the prophecy of Isaiah:

Behold, the Lord's hand is not shortened,
That it cannot save;
Nor his ear heavy,
That it cannot hear.
But your iniquities have separated you from your God;
And your sins have hidden his face from you,
So that he will not hear

(Isa. 59:1-2).

Scripture also tells us God does not hear the prayers of the unforgiving (Mark 11:25-26), or of the selfish (James 4:3).

Does this not explain why many of our so-called 'prayers' are not answered? The Lord is not obligated to hear our prayers if we are treating his laws casually.

Does this mean we have to be perfect before we can expect

God to answer our prayers? If it did, there would never be an answered prayer in this world, because there is no such thing as a perfect Christian this side of eternity. We should, therefore, understand this teaching to mean that the Christian will take the laws of God seriously, diligently strive to keep them and, when he fails, will be truly repentant.

Praying according to the will of God

As we go about this business of comparing Scripture with Scripture, we shall at length find one passage that seems to be very clear indeed, and we should interpret those that are less clear in the light of it. That passage is 1 John 5:14-15.

We need to keep in mind that the apostle John wrote these words. He was one of Jesus' original disciples. He was present when Jesus gave all the prayer promises we have already looked at. And here is his understanding of all of them: 'If we ask anything according to his will, he hears us. And if we know that he hears us, whatever we ask, we know that we have the petitions that we have asked of him.'

Those verses, then, that tell us our prayers will be granted on the condition that we have enough faith (Matt. 21:21-22; Mark 11:22-24; James 5:13-15) still assume that what we ask for is according to the will of God.

As far as many are concerned, we might as well not pray at all if we have to pray according to the will of God. If God wills something, what is the point of praying for it? The answer to that question is that the God who wills various things is also the God who has appointed prayer as one of the means by which he implements his will.

Lest we feel too constricted by having to pray according to the will of God, we need to keep the following truths firmly in mind:

1. The will of God is far greater than most of us have ever realized. If we feel limited by praying according to the will of God, we need to open our Bibles and get acquainted with the vastness of God's will.

2. Praying according to the will of God does not put any restrictions upon our asking. We may ask God for whatever is good and legitimate, but we must realize he is only obligated to do what he has promised.

God's people are to be a praying people. One of the main sources of strength for our travelling here is to be in continuing communication with our headquarters in heaven. We shall not have the will to do so if we have drawn false conclusions from the prayer promises and have allowed our false conclusions to disillusion us. If we remember that prayer was not given to us so that we can get our will done in heaven, but rather so that we can get God's will done on earth, we shall find it to be the source of strength we so urgently need while we travel home.

14.
The promise of God's sustaining care

Psalm 55:22

The Christian is embarrassed with riches because he has, in the words of the apostle Peter, been blessed with 'exceedingly great and precious promises' (2 Peter 1:4).

The promise before us is one of the most familiar and most loved of all. It comes at the close of a chapter in which David was distressed over a great personal crisis. What was the nature of this crisis? Many think it was the deep emotional distress he felt when his beloved son, Absalom, tried to wrest the throne from him.

Whatever the nature of David's crisis, this much is clear: the Holy Spirit of God compelled him to write a promise that has helped and blessed the children of God down through the centuries.

A fundamental reality

There are three things about this promise that cry for our attention. The first and most obvious aspect is that it deals with a fundamental reality of Christian living, namely, being burdened.

Every child of God knows what it is to be burdened in some way or other. What is a burden? It is something that loads us down and causes us to be distressed and to feel that we are at the end of our resources. It is something that presses in upon us and gives us a feeling of heaviness.

When we hear of burdens, we automatically think in terms of specific afflictions and trials. Sickness, loss of a loved one, loss of employment, loss of a friendship — these are all common burdens that most of us have to bear at one time or another. And sometimes we find ourselves bearing several of these burdens at once.

But we should not think of burdens only in terms of specific crises or afflictions. We can also be burdened by the general responsibilities and cares of life. There are times when there is nothing especially wrong, but we just feel that family, church and career obligations are too much for us.

There is, however, something more in this word 'burden' than experiencing a specific affliction or feeling the general cares of life. This word can also be translated 'gift'. Derek Kidner writes, 'The word burden is too restrictive: it means whatever is given you, your appointed lot.'[1]

A burden as a gift? To many that sounds something like a square circle. We want to think it has to be one thing or the other. If something is a burden, it is no gift; if something is a gift, it is no burden. But the Bible makes it clear that God does indeed give us burdens to bear.

Those who have trouble with this are the ones who think the Lord's purpose is to make sure our lives are smooth and easy. To them a burden is *prima facie* evidence that God has failed. The truth is, however, that the Lord has a far different purpose for us than simply making sure life is easy. His purpose is to cause us to mature and grow into his likeness, and this requires him to wean us away from the world's thinking and doing and bring us to lean upon his grace. Giving burdens to his children is an indispensable element in achieving this purpose.

A vital distinction

The second feature of this promise that demands our attention is that it deals with the burden-bearer and not with the burden.

We all have a tendency to read into Scripture what we want to find there, and it is very easy for us to do so with this promise. When we are burdened, we are interested in one thing, and one thing alone: getting rid of whatever it is that is burdening us, and the sooner the better!

So we want this promise to say the Lord will remove our burden, or carry it for us. But look again and you will find it says no such thing. It speaks rather of the Lord sustaining us and not allowing us to be moved. The promise, then, is not to take the burden but to sustain the burden-bearer. The promise is not that the *burden* will be moved but rather that the *righteous* will not be moved. If, on the other hand, the burden were taken away, there would be no need for us to be sustained.

There can be no doubt, of course, that God can remove those things that burden and distress us. One word from him and they would be gone. And there are plenty of instances in which he has removed burdens and problems. But the general rule is that God does not remove the burden until we learn to carry it with his sustaining grace.

The Lord will sustain us

Let's look at the two parts of this promise. First, what does it mean when the Lord says he will sustain us? It means he will support and strengthen us while we carry the burden. To understand why the Lord does this all we have to do is think of a parent whose child is learning to ride a bike. The parent does not ride the bike for the child. But neither does the parent leave the child to himself. Instead he strikes the middle course.

He lets the child ride the bike himself and he lends just enough support and help to keep the child from calamity. Why does the parent take this course? Wouldn't it be much easier for him to simply ride the bike for the child? Yes, but the child would never reach maturity if the parent did everything for him.

The righteous will not be moved

That brings us to the second part of the promise, the part which says the Lord will not allow the righteous to be moved. Does it not seem as if this part of the promise has failed? Are there not plenty of instances of people who claimed to be trusting the Lord who seem to have been moved or shaken by the burdens they had to bear?

We need to understand that the Lord is talking about the righteous being moved in an ultimate sense. He is not saying the righteous will never be distressed over a burden. That would destroy the whole purpose of this promise, which is to deal with the distress of the righteous. David was deeply distressed as he wrote the words of this chapter. He says, 'I am restless in my complaint' (v. 2); 'My heart is severely pained within me' (v. 4); and 'Fearfulness and trembling have come upon me' (v. 5).

When the Lord says the righteous will not be moved, he is speaking in the ultimate sense that they will not be so shaken as to finally lose their faith in God. The great Charles Spurgeon says of the righteous person carrying a heavy burden: 'He may move like the boughs of a tree in the tempest, but he shall never be moved like a tree torn up by the roots.'[2]

The apostle Paul had to bear more burdens in a year than most of us will ever have in a lifetime, and he was able to write, 'We are ... struck down, but not destroyed' (2 Cor. 4:8-9). In other words, Paul was knocked down but not knocked out. So it is with each child of God and his or her burdens.

A clear condition

That brings us to a final feature of this promise. We should note that it contains a condition.

Are you burdened today? Do you want to receive the Lord's strength and support? Do you want to feel this confidence that the burden is not going ultimately to defeat you, that you will not finally be moved? David tells you what to do. He says you must 'cast your burden on the Lord'.

What does it mean to 'cast' our burden on the Lord? David gives us the answer in verses 16 and 17 of this psalm. He says:

As for me, I will call upon God...
Evening and morning and at noon
I will pray, and cry aloud,
And he shall hear my voice.

To cast our burden on the Lord means to tell him about it. Have you talked to the Lord about your burden? No, he probably will not remove it from you. When you give it to him, the chances are that he will give it right back to you. But, thank God, he will give you something to go with it: that sustaining grace he has promised.

This was the experience of the apostle Paul. He had a terrible burden to bear that he called his 'thorn in the flesh', and three times he went to the Lord to ask for it to be removed. The Lord refused to remove the burden, but he did give Paul these sustaining words: 'My grace is sufficient for you, for my strength is made perfect in weakness' (2 Cor. 12:9).

Talk to the Lord then. Tell him about that burden that weighs you down. Tell him of the difficulty you have in trusting his kind purpose towards you. Tell him of your deep need for his strength and support. Acknowledge him to be the giver of the burden and ask him to help you grow in grace as a result of it. Thank him for loving you enough to send these maturing burdens into your life. And trust him to send that sustaining grace that you earnestly pray for.

No one had more burdens to bear than the Lord Jesus Christ himself. Such a statement sounds strange to many. They have the notion that Christ's humanity was like a kind of suit that he 'zipped on', that it was not a real humanity. But the Bible assures us that while Jesus was fully God, he was also fully man. He was the God-man. Part of the human experience is carrying burdens and, oh, what burdens Christ carried!

Look at how Christ carried his burdens. Time after time we see him casting them on the Lord. He was a man of prayer who constantly cast his burdens upon the Father. Luke tells us he often went into the wilderness to pray (Luke 5:16); that he continued all night in prayer to God (Luke 6:12); and that he urged his disciples to pray with these words: 'Men always ought to pray and not lose heart...' (Luke 18:1).

May God help us to follow his example and, in so doing, not only to find strength for the carrying of our burdens but also to demonstrate the difference between believers and unbelievers. Unbelievers have their burdens too, but only the children of God have the sustaining grace of a loving heavenly Father to draw from when they face the burdens of life. As unbelievers see us drawing from that grace they will be convinced that there is something to our faith.

15.
The promise of perfect peace

Isaiah 26:3-4

The prophet Isaiah brought a message that was both sombre and joyful. The sombre part was that his people would see their capital, Jerusalem, and its glorious temple devastated and destroyed, and most of them would be carried away into captivity in Babylon. The joyful part of the message was that the destruction of Judah and the captivity of its citizens would not be the end of the story. God promised that the people would eventually be released from their captivity, that they would return to their homeland and that they would rebuild their city and their temple.

In this chapter of Isaiah's prophecy we find the prophet strumming this joyful chord. He looks beyond the sin of the nation and the consequent judgement trembling on the horizon to that glad day of restoration, and he bursts out in a song of celebration. This is a song of prophecy. It would be the song the people themselves would sing when their captivity was finally over and their city was at last rebuilt. With this song the people would rejoice over the strength of their restored city, strength that would come not from its mighty walls but from their mighty God (v. 1). This was the very same God who would have been their security before the Babylonians came in, if they had only been willing to renounce their idols and serve him.

Even though this song was given to the people of Judah in the historical context I have described, it is rich in meaning and comfort for us as well, and this is especially true of the two verses before us. There is, if I may put it in this way, a glorious indistinctiveness in these verses. Do you see it? The Lord will keep *him* in perfect peace whose mind is stayed upon God. To whom does 'him' refer? Does it apply only to the individual Jews of that day? No, thank God, there is no limitation or restriction here. Anyone of any age may wriggle into this indistinctiveness and enjoy the perfect peace this promise deals with.

There are three distinct and discernible parts to this promise.

A precious commodity

First, note the precious and rare commodity this promise offers: perfect peace. What kind of peace is the prophet talking about? The Christian is one who has peace with God. He has that rest of soul that we considered earlier. But here Isaiah is dealing with a different kind of peace — the kind that gives us freedom from agitation and anxiety over the trials and afflictions of life. The peace Isaiah is talking about is the same kind of peace we find Paul talking about: 'Be anxious for nothing, but in everything by prayer and supplication, with thanksgiving, let your requests be made known to God; and the peace of God, which surpasses all understanding, will guard your hearts and minds through Christ Jesus' (Phil. 4:6-7). It is that same peace the psalmist mentions in Psalm 112:7. There he says of the righteous: 'He will not be afraid of evil tidings; his heart is steadfast, trusting in the Lord.'

Every Christian knows being at peace with God does not automatically entail being free from anxiety. This is the reason why Jesus constantly warned his disciples about being anxious and worrying (Matt. 6:25-34).

Christians are called upon to live out their faith in a world of peace-wreckers. *People* can wreck our peace: that troublesome marriage partner, that demanding employer, those unruly children, those annoying neighbours. Then there are peace-wrecking *circumstances*: a society that wages unrelenting war on our values, that nagging illness that makes life uncertain and each day a burden, those bills that pile up ever faster. On top of all that there are peace-wrecking *imaginations*: 'What if I come down with this dreadful disease? What if I cannot make ends meet when I retire? What if my children rebel against God?' Even *desires* can wreck our peace. We can spend so much time yearning for something we do not have — a possession, a promotion, prestige — that we do not enjoy what we do have.

In a world like this we often hear people say they would like to have 'just a little peace now and then'. The great thing about this text is that it offers us not just a little peace but 'perfect peace'. As a matter of fact, the word 'perfect' is not in the Hebrew text. There the phrase simply reads: 'You will keep him in peace, peace whose mind is stayed on you.' Charles Spurgeon notes that this was the Hebrew way of 'expressing emphatic peace; true and real peace; double peace; peace of great depth and vast extent'.[1]

In other words, the promise offers a peace sufficient for all that life throws at us. No, it does not offer us a perfect life or perfect circumstances, but a perfect peace in the midst of a difficult life and trying circumstances.

It is important that we understand this. Sometimes people seem to assume that being a Christian means a person should have no serious problems. As soon as one of God's people encounters suffering in some form or fashion, there always seems to be someone there to say, 'I thought you were a Christian. Why is this happening to you?' The implication is, of course, that there is nothing to Christianity, or Christians would not suffer.

The thing that separates the Christian from others, how-ever, is not that he has no difficulties or problems, but rather that he has a strength and a peace in the midst of the difficulties.

The source of peace

But let's turn our attention now to consider the source of this peace. The Authorized Version translates what the prophets say on this point in this way: 'For in the LORD JEHOVAH is everlasting strength.' The New King James Version puts it like this: 'For in YAH, the LORD, is everlasting strength.'

The word 'YAH' is an abridged form of JEHOVAH. So what we have here then is Isaiah duplicating the name of God. He literally says we can have 'peace, peace' because of our 'LORD, LORD'. Albert Barnes says this duplication of the name of God 'seems designed to express, in the highest sense possible, the majesty, glory, and holiness of God; to excite the highest possible reverence where language fails of completely con-veying the idea'.[2]

In addition to duplicating the name of God, Isaiah goes on to assert that he has 'everlasting strength'. It is interesting that the prophet moves from our need, through perfect peace, to the everlasting strength of the Lord.

Why do we have anxiety? Isn't it because we realize that much of life is out of our control, that we have no power to change circumstances and direct events?

God is under no such limitations. He is the God of everlast-ing strength. For just a small impression of how great is the Lord's strength, all we have to do is read the fortieth chapter of Isaiah's prophecy. There we find Isaiah struggling to convey something of God's greatness. He compares him with the biggest, the wisest, the strongest, the shrewdest, the noblest and the highest, and finds that all pale in comparison to the majestic, sovereign God of eternity.

The condition

That brings us finally to deal with the condition that is attached to this promise. The prophet says, 'You will keep him in perfect peace, whose mind is stayed on you.'

Notice first that this statement deals with 'staying' ourselves 'on' God. What does it mean to stay ourselves on something? It means to lean on it for support. It is to fix or establish something as a foundation and to rest our weight on it. To stay ourselves on God, then, is to lean upon him for support, or to rest upon him as the foundation for our lives.

How do we go about staying ourselves on God? Notice that Isaiah's statement also deals with the mind. Our minds are to be stayed upon God. In other words, our minds are to be supported by God's truth. Staying our minds on God means fixing and settling our minds on his truth and not being blown about by the latest fad and the newest teaching.

This staying our minds on God's truth is to be a continuous, ongoing action. Here is where many of us make a mistake. We want to wait until some crisis springs upon us before we start staying ourselves on God's truth, and we often find little comfort. The key is to stay our minds on God's truth on a daily basis. That will not only bring deep peace and joy into our daily lives but it will also give us a fixed reference-point to turn to when we are confronted with a crisis.

It is also important for us to realize that the staying of our minds on God's truth must be complete, or whole. When we lean ourselves on something for support, we do not reap the full benefit of it unless we wholly lean on it. Many Christians make the mistake of leaning only part of their minds on the Word of God. They believe parts of it, but they also subscribe in part to the humanistic thinking of our age. Thinking there is some darkness in the Bible's light and some light in the world's darkness, they fail to lean wholly on the Word of God and so do not fully realize the peace of God.

If we want the perfect peace of this promise, then, we must make sure we are continually and completely resting ourselves on the truth of God's Word. How blessed is the person who does this! The trials of life cannot shake his peace because, fortified with the Word of God, he knows that all the trials that come his way are for his good and God's glory (Rom. 8:28). Even death itself cannot shake him, because he knows his citizenship is in heaven (Phil. 3:20-21) and, like Paul, he is confident that to be absent from the body is to be present with the Lord (2 Cor. 5:6-8).

The Lord Jesus was pre-eminently a man of peace. He was always unruffled and calm, no matter what his circumstances and no matter how extreme or harsh the provocation. Jesus was never 'stressed out', to use a term often used today, although he had plenty of reasons to be. He experienced continual interruptions and intrusions. He carried the awesome burden of sharing the sorrows and hurts of those to whom he ministered. He endured the hostility of his enemies. But with it all, Jesus showed no trace of nervousness, irritability, or being 'on edge'.

Look closely at the life of Jesus and you will see the key to his peace. It is the very thing Isaiah emphasizes. Jesus was 'stayed' upon God the Father. His mind was totally absorbed with, and focused on, the Word of God. We only have to look at his temptations in the wilderness to see his utter reliance on the Word of God. There he met each of Satan's temptations by saying, 'It is written...' (Matt. 4:4,7,10).

The Christian who follows his Lord's example will have his Lord's peace. Yes, the Christian who is stayed on the Word of God still faces real trials that bring real hurt into his life, but the hurt cannot drown the perfect peace that is his, and he finds himself singing in the midst of the pain:

Every joy or trial falleth from above,
Traced upon our dial by the Sun of love;
We may trust him fully all for us to do;
They who trust him wholly find him wholly true.
Stayed upon Jehovah, hearts are fully blessed.
Finding, as he promised, perfect peace and rest.

16.
God's promise to meet our needs

Philippians 4:19

We tend to make the promises of God too wide or too narrow. We do the first when we apply promises to people, situations and circumstances they were never intended to cover. We do the second when we so restrict and qualify the promises that nothing is left of them.

The result of making the promises too wide is disillusion-ment. When we try to stretch promises to cover what they were never intended to cover, they simply do not come true, and then we conclude God has failed and cannot be trusted. Many people are resentful towards God because they think he has failed them, but the real failure came when they thought God had promised them something when in fact he had not done so.

The result of making the promises too narrow is loss of the blessings that they offer. A severely reduced or limited prom-ise does not excite us even to desire its fulfilment, let alone to expect it.

The promise before us presents us with a real challenge on this matter of width. On one hand, we have the apostle Paul promising the Philippians that God would meet all their needs. This has been taken as a promise to all of God's people of all ages. On the other hand, we have no trouble finding Christians who appear to be in great need. Some are ill. Some are poor. Some, especially in foreign lands, go without proper food and shelter.

Even Paul himself admitted he had learned 'to suffer need' (v. 12) just before he promised the Philippians that God would supply all their need. And Paul knew what he was talking about when he referred to experiencing need. Read his second letter to the Corinthians and you will find a long list of things he suffered in his ministry, including weariness (he needed rest), sleeplessness (he needed sleep), hunger (he needed food) and cold (he needed shelter) (2 Cor. 11:27). Now here is the great question: how could a man who had experienced so much need promise the Philippians that God would supply all their needs?

How are we to resolve this dilemma? Are we merely to say Paul suffered all these things because he lacked faith in God? (This is, in fact, how many today would get around the problem. Whenever a Christian is ill, or financially distressed, they are very quick to say he or she has simply failed to trust God.) Or do we say Paul suffered need, and Christians today suffer need, because the promise is counterfeit? The answer is to recognize both the limitations which surround the promise and how wide it is.

The limitations surrounding the promise

We need first to see that there are certain boundaries around the promise that limit it.

One boundary is that *it applies only to those who are Christians*. Paul says God supplies needs 'by Christ Jesus'. As we have noted, Christ is the one through whom we have all the promises. He receives them from God the Father and then conveys them to his people. If we do not have Christ, we cannot expect to benefit from any of God's promises.

Another boundary that restricts the promise is that *it deals only with our needs, not with our wants*. Most of us are not very skilled in distinguishing between the two. We think we do not need the things that in fact we do need, and we think we need the very things we do not. Every parent knows what this is all about. Children are experts at confusing what they need with what they want, and the parent sometimes has to deny the child what he wants in order to give him what he needs. We can be very much like immature children with God and start demanding that he supply our wants but, in the words of Warren Wiersbe, 'God has not promised to supply all our greeds.'[1]

It would have been easy for Paul to have been confused over this point of mistaking wants for needs. Here he was, the foremost spokesman for the Christian faith, writing to the Philippians from a prison cell. From a mere human perspective it would seem his greatest need was to be released from prison so the progress of the churches would not be put in jeopardy. But the Lord had other plans, and Paul knew the Lord's plans are always best.

A third boundary to keep in mind is *the difference between feeling a need and having the need supplied.* The promise does not say the Philippians would never feel a need, but rather that God would supply their need. No doubt Paul felt a need for a while in that prison cell, but God supplied that need. The Philippians sent him a gift by the hand of Epaphroditus (Phil. 2:25; 4:18). The gift itself met one need and Epaphroditus met another: the need for companionship and fellowship.

The important point here is that the Lord did not prevent Paul from experiencing a need, but he supplied the need. A need has to exist in order for it to be supplied. We tend to think, if we have a need, that the Lord has failed us, but the promise does not say we shall never feel a need. The Lord lets us feel need for a while and then meets it in his own time and way.

There is one more boundary for us to keep in mind. I have already indicated that the promise applies only to Christians. I must go on to say the context of the promise suggests *a condition Christians themselves must meet.*

Keep in mind that Paul wrote this promise to the Philippians shortly after they sent their gift. In effect, then, Paul says, 'You supplied my need and now you may rest assured that God will meet yours.' In other words, I am suggesting that even we who are Christians should not automatically expect God to meet our needs if we are unwilling to be used by God to meet the needs of others. God is gracious and often supplies our needs even when we are not serving him as we ought, but he is under no obligation to bless a disobedient child.

The Lord Jesus stated essentially the same principle when he said, 'Give, and it will be given to you, good measure, pressed down, shaken together, and running over will be put into your bosom. For with the same measure that you use, it will be measured back to you' (Luke 6:38).

Paul expressed a similar principle to the Corinthians: 'He who sows sparingly will also reap sparingly, and he who sows bountifully will also reap bountifully' (2 Cor. 9:6).

In another place, the Lord Jesus promised his disciples that their heavenly Father would meet their basic needs, but he also included a condition: 'But seek first the kingdom of God and his righteousness, and all these things will be added to you' (Matt. 6:33). We want God to do the adding, but we often fail to do the seeking.

All of these things show us there definitely are limitations to the promise. Many find this hard to accept. They think any restriction renders the promise worthless and leaves only an empty shell. Thank God, this is not the case.

How wide the promise is

The apostle refers to God's 'riches in glory', or his glorious riches. God's riches are so great that they remain undiminished even when he meets the needs of his children. Out of these riches God gives to his children in splendid or magnificent fashion.

Sometimes he gives us a blessing by taking the need away. At other times he does not take it away, but gives us strength so we can bear it. Paul experienced both of these types of giving. Eventually the Lord delivered him from his imprisonment, but before he was delivered he was given strength to face the hardship of it all. So Paul was able to thank the Lord for giving him both the strength to face prison and, finally, deliverance from it. To Timothy he wrote, 'But the Lord stood with me and strengthened me... And I was delivered out of the mouth of the lion' (2 Tim. 4:17).

The psalmist celebrated these same two aspects of how God meets our needs when he wrote, 'For by you I can run against a troop, and by my God I can leap over a wall' (Ps. 18:29). Sometimes God causes us to leap over the wall of our need. At other times he gives us strength to run through a whole troop of need. Either way we experience his riches.

We prefer leaping over the wall, of course. We want God to meet our need by delivering us from it. But we should never minimize the blessing of God strengthening us in the midst of need. Paul found that to be such a great blessing that he was able to say, 'I can do all things through Christ who strengthens me' (Phil. 4:13).

This finally is the answer to our original question. How could Paul experience so much need and still promise the Philippians that God would supply their need? He had experienced God's supply, sometimes in God's eventual removal of his needs, but always in God's giving him strength to face them.

So this promise is very wide. Do you doubt it? Look again at those words, 'by Christ Jesus'. There is the final proof both of the riches of God and of his willingness to use them on our behalf. The Lord Jesus came all the way from heaven's glory to Calvary's pain and agony, and he did it all that we might be saved. If God would go to this length to supply our greatest need, that of salvation, we should never doubt his willingness to supply our lesser needs.

What should our response be to this appropriately narrow yet amply wide promise? Isn't it obvious? We should stop worrying and fretting over the basic needs of life and give ourselves, as Jesus said, to seeking God's kingdom and righteousness. In other words, we should substitute life's greatest concern for all our little concerns.

Most of us have a great deal of trouble here. We seem unable to keep ourselves from worrying over life's basic needs. When we have nothing else to worry about, we worry about worrying too much. As one writer put it, 'I've joined the new "Don't Worry Club" and now I hold my breath. I'm so afraid I'll worry that I'm almost worried to death.'[2]

Joel Gregory shows the way to defeat worry with the following story: 'One of those daring early pilots was circum-navigating the globe in his tiny airplane. Some 2,000 miles out to sea, away from any sort of land, he heard a gnawing somewhere under his cockpit. As he listened, he realized that it was a rat gnawing away at the wires and the insulation of the plane. And he realized that he was in big trouble. What could he do? Then he remembered that rats are subterranean or terrestrial creatures. So he flew the plane a thousand feet higher, then another, and another until he was up to 20,000 feet. The gnawing stopped. When he reached the end of his journey and finally landed, he found a dead rat under the floor of his cockpit.'

Then Gregory makes this application: 'The rat had been gnawing away at his very lifeline. But what did the pilot do? He found that when he lifted the whole situation into another atmosphere, literally, the threat of the rat that was worrying him was removed. Jesus says we need to move into another atmosphere — a calm, confident trust, the kind that little children have, toward the heavenly Father.'[3]

17.
The promise of a refuge and a strength

Psalm 46:1-5

Earthquakes are rare in most parts of the world, but 'heartquakes' are as common as the sniffles in winter. A 'heartquake' is when our hearts tremble with fear over some real or imagined threat. I will not go as far as to say Christians should never experience a heartquake, but I do suggest that they should know how to treat themselves when they feel the onslaught of fear, and they should be able to find relief from it.

Most of the psalms were penned by David, but this psalm seems to have been written many years after his time and added to the collection of his psalms. John R. W. Stott writes, 'The situation envisaged in the psalm, together with its resemblance in metaphor and phrase to some of Isaiah's prophecies suggest the overthrow of Sennacherib's army in 701 B.C.'[1]

That overthrow came about as a result of the Lord's sovereign intervention on behalf of the people of Judah. Sennacherib had surrounded the city with his great army. Boasting that he had made King Hezekiah and the people of Jerusalem 'like a caged bird', Sennacherib demanded surrender. This bleak situation appeared to be hopeless, but Isaiah spoke this comforting word from God to Hezekiah: 'I will defend this city, to save it for my own sake and for my servant

David's sake' (2 Kings 19:34).The threat ended when the angel of the Lord went into the Assyrian camp and killed a great multitude (2 Kings 19:35-36).

The author of this psalm knew, then, what it was to experience fear, but he also knew some truths that had the power to alleviate fear. In this psalm he speaks of God as an unshakeable refuge (vv. 1-3) and as a sustaining river (vv. 4-5).

God, the unshakeable refuge

Perhaps the best way to deal with fear is to imagine the worst scenario possible and seek to determine where that would leave us. That appears to be what this psalmist did. He goes out of his way to paint calamity in its blackest shades. He takes the two most stable and unchangeable things he could think of, earth and the mountains, and the most restless and menacing force he could think of, the sea, and lays them over against each other. What if the earth were removed? What if the mountains should slip into the midst of the sea? What if all that is stable and dependable should suddenly be swallowed up in turbulence and turmoil? What if everything that is nailed down suddenly comes loose? What then?

This is an entirely different approach from anything that most of us have ever contemplated. We constantly assume that nothing will ever drastically change our world.

Some time ago I heard a radio phone-in programme on the topic of investments. The gentleman who was fielding the questions suggested that if investors wanted real security they should invest in government programmes. When he was quizzed on his preference for this particular type of investment, he said the government will always be here. He had obviously never allowed for the possibility that nations can pass away.

The man who wrote this psalm had a depth of discernment most of us never attain. He proposes a radical principle in this matter of coping with fear: shake everything that can be shaken, see what you have left, and live on the basis of that.

That sounds all very well and good in theory, but how did it work out for this man? What did he end up with? 'God', he says in defiant tones, 'is our refuge and strength, a very present help in trouble' (v. 1). Furthermore he says, 'The Lord of hosts is with us; the God of Jacob is our refuge' (vv. 7,11).

Do you see what he is saying? Allow me to put words in his mouth: 'Take it all away, let the earth be destroyed and the mountains slip into the heart of the sea, and you have not really even touched me. My peace does not depend on the continuation of this life as I have known it. My all is not invested in this life, but in God who is my refuge. When the mountains and earth are gone, my refuge will still be there.'

This does not mean that we suddenly have no problems, that the difficulties just vanish away. Such an interpretation would fly in the face of everything this psalm is talking about. The point of the psalm is that we have a refuge or shelter in the midst of the difficulty. No matter how painful our circumstances, or how uncertain our future, we may rely upon the truths proclaimed in this psalm: God is, God is with us, God is with us to help us and God's purposes will not fail.

We read these truths and immediately leap to the conclusion that God is under an obligation to do for us exactly what we want done. And if he does not do it, we conclude that he has failed to help us. We must never lose sight of the fact that God's ways are far greater than our ways, and he helps us when we are often totally unaware of it. This psalm calls us away from being absorbed with our own minuscule corner of the universe and asks us to focus on the much larger purposes of God.

Martin Luther's hymn, 'A Mighty Fortress is Our God,' is

based on this psalm, and it accurately reflects what the psalmist had in mind:

> Let goods and kindred go,
> This mortal life also;
> The body they may kill:
> God's truth abideth still,
> His kingdom is for ever.

So the first thing we must do if we are to combat fear is to
fix our eyes on the God who unfailingly keeps and shelters us
in the midst of difficult circumstances.

God, the sustaining river

But that is only half the story. The psalmist is not content
simply to refer to God as our sheltering refuge. He goes on to
call attention to God as our sustaining river (vv. 4-5).

At that time all the cities were walled, and it was exceedingly difficult for an enemy to break through. It was common,
therefore, for armies to simply surround the city and wait for
the inhabitants to run out of food and water. The water was
really the more critical of the two. If a city did not have a good
water supply, it was in real trouble.

The city of Jerusalem was extremely vulnerable at this
point until King Hezekiah constructed the Siloam tunnel. This
tunnel gave the city an abundant supply of water and prevented
enemies from using the strategy I mentioned. The fact that this
psalm makes mention of a river that makes glad the city of God
(v. 4) is one of the prime indications that it was written after
Hezekiah built his famous tunnel.

Now here is the point the psalmist was concerned to make:
God is to his people like that river was to the city. Just as that

river was there to sustain the city, so God is present to sustain us.

When we set this picture of God alongside the other, God as our refuge, we have all we need to defeat the spectre of fear. It is wonderful to have God as our refuge, but we also need him as our river. It would have been of no value to the people of that time to have a fort to hide in if there was nothing in that fort to keep them alive. They had to have the sustenance along with the shelter.

What does all this have to do with us as we seek to cope with fear? Let me put it like this — what we feed is what grows. If we feed our fears we may be assured that they will become monstrous indeed. But if we feed faith, the opposite of fear, our faith will grow and our fears will begin to shrink.

Some Christians are never able to overcome fear in the midst of a crisis because they have never understood a basic principle — we must keep our spiritual strength up before the crisis comes. The river was to be used not just in time of crisis, but to sustain everyday life. If we are drawing strength from God on a daily basis, we shall find it natural to do so in a crisis.

The truth is that most of us want God to be with us in the crisis, but we fail adequately to nurture our relationship with him before the crisis comes. We want him to be there to deliver us from our fear, but we do not want to do those things that will make our faith strong.

And what are those things that make faith strong? There can be no shortcuts here. God has appointed certain means by which we receive our spiritual sustenance. They are Bible study, prayer, regular worship in the house of God and fellowship with the people of God. You can mark this down — your faith will never grow strong if you neglect these things.

Fear is at epidemic proportions today, and many find themselves unable to cope. The Christian, however, has a resource. As he travels life's pathway, he can draw strength from knowing God is his refuge and his river. The Christian knows that, no matter how great his problems, his God is sufficient for him.

How do we know these things to be true? Claiming something to be true does not make it true. Many would have no hesitation in asserting that Christians claim God to be their unshakeable refuge and sustaining river merely because they want to think of him in these ways.

Was this the case with the psalmist? Was he indulging in some wishful thinking, or was there more to it than that? As we have noted, the psalmist had solid evidence for claiming God as a refuge and a river. He could refer to an event in history that proved the sufficiency of God for his people. Sennacherib had threatened the city, the Lord had promised to defend the city and Sennacherib was sent packing. No more proof was needed of God's sufficiency.

Christians can triumphantly assert the sufficiency of God for life's trials and crises from even firmer historical evidence. When the angel announced the birth of Jesus to Joseph, he said his name would be be called Immanuel, which means 'God with us' (Matt. 1:23). How can we ever doubt the sufficiency of God for us when he has given his own Son? The presence of Christ in human history triumphantly trumpets the truth that God himself has come among us to be 'a very present help'. His coming to dwell among us assures us that we can find in God an unshakeable refuge to protect us in the midst of life's trials and, thank God, to protect us from hell itself in the life to come. The presence of Christ assures us that we have in God a river. We can draw sustaining grace from him each day of our lives.

18.
The promise of
the church's triumph

Matthew 16:13-19

She is one of the great loves of my life. I love her so much that I lavish my time and my money on her. I love her so much that I look forward to being with her. I love her so much that I would be willing to die for her. She is the mother of my children. She is beautiful beyond description to me, more beautiful now than that blessed day when she first gleamed on my sight.

Yes, all of these things are true of my wonderful wife, but I am not talking about her, but about the church of the Lord Jesus Christ. Yes, she is one of my great loves. Yes, she is the mother of my children — my sons after the flesh became children of God through her faithful proclamation of the gospel. Yes, she is beautiful to me and she becomes more and more beautiful to me with each passing day. Yes, I would lay down my very life for her. I love the church of Jesus Christ with every fibre of my heart and with every ounce of my devotion.

I am so glad Jesus has a church. I am so glad to be a part of her. I am so glad that I do not have to fret about her future because I have a promise from the Lord Jesus himself that his church will be secure for ever.

Look with me at this promise. Turn it over in your mind. Draw the nectar of comfort from it. Rest upon it. Rejoice in it.

The glory of the church

First, think with me about what a glorious thing the church of Jesus Christ is. Old theologians used to divide the church into two parts: the church militant and the church triumphant. The latter consists of all those believers who have gone on to be with the Lord. Their battle is over and their rest has begun. They know nothing now of struggle, hardship and heartache, but are in a state of perfect rest. However, we are part of the church militant. We are still in this world of turmoil and struggle.

In either expression, the church is glorious beyond words. She is a spiritual building which is composed of individual Christians. We were placed in this building by the grace of God. It was his grace that found us in the quarry of humanity. It was his grace that lifted us out of that quarry, that broke us and hewed us. It was his grace that made us living stones and placed us in the church.

The church is glorious because of that grace. We no more deserved to be part of the church than any of the other materials in the human quarry. We were sinners like all the rest. We had broken God's holy law and were deserving only of his wrath and condemnation. But this unspeakable, matchless grace of God sent the Lord Jesus Christ to Calvary's cross. There he received in his own person the penalty that was rightfully ours. There he shed his blood for us. In the words of the apostle Paul, 'Christ ... loved the church and gave himself for it.'

Now the church belongs to him. She is his purchased and prized possession and he has a purpose for her. She is now to show forth his praises (1 Peter 2:9-10).

The church, then, is glorious because of the quarry from which she was taken (the quarry of sin), because of the grace that purchased her and because of the purpose the Lord has for her.

Satan's hatred of the church

How we should rejoice in the church! How we should glory in her! But not everyone does rejoice in her. Not everyone loves her. Turn with me now from this glorious picture of the grace of God that has taken us from the quarry of sin and made us part of this spiritual house, the church. Turn with me to look at a very dark and sombre truth, namely, the deep hatred Satan has for the church.

Satan hates the church with a hatred as great as the greatest love the church has ever known — the love of Christ. He hates her intensely and fervently. He hates her because he lost her. He once had dominion over every member of the church, as he does now over all who do not belong to God. Each member of the church was part of his quarry, and the Lord Jesus came and took them away from him.

Satan also hates the church because she stands for everything he hates. We have already noted that the Lord has a purpose for the church. She is to demonstrate the glory of redemption and to show the utter folly of living for Satan. She is to be pure and righteous and holy, and all of this makes her despicable in Satan's eyes.

Because he hates her so passionately, Satan is ever busy seeking to destroy her. Jesus speaks here of the gates of hell. All the cities of that day had high walls and gates. The gates were the means of entering or leaving the city. The truth that Jesus was conveying when he spoke of 'the gates of hell' is of Satan sitting in his headquarters — hell — and sending out through the gates every device and strategy imaginable to destroy the church.

False doctrine is one of the most dangerous things the church can ever face. Where does it come from? Right out of the gates of hell from Satan himself!

Hypocrisy is another terrible danger for the church. When professing Christians show by their lives that they are not what they profess to be, the world laughs at the church and ridicules her message. Where does hypocrisy come from? It is a plot hatched in hell itself and sent out from its gates.

Dissension in the church, persecution, apathy, selfishness, childishness, anger and resentment, a critical, harsh spirit — name anything that hinders rather than helps the church, that slows her steps and chills her spirit, that divides her attention, that saps her energy, and you can be sure that it was spawned in hell amidst demonic shrieks of joy, and sent out through the gates upon an unsuspecting church.

Here we have, then, a glorious church that is hated by hell and assaulted with every demonic, hellish device imaginable. It is hard for Christians sitting comfortably in a worship service to comprehend, but, believe it or not, there is a cosmic struggle swirling around the church of Christ. Every time the church comes together for worship, heaven and hell join in battle. Every time the church goes out to minister in this lost world, hell itself resists her.

The security of the church

What will be the outcome of this battle? Sometimes it has appeared that the church was on her last legs and about to breathe her last. Thank God, we do not need to trouble ourselves about the final outcome of this struggle. We have a promise from the Lord Jesus that tells us what a firm foundation the church has and how wonderfully secure she is.

We have no need to worry about the church because she is built on an invincible, indestructible rock. What or who is this rock? Is it Simon Peter? We would do well to tremble if the church were built on any mere man. Thank God, the foundation is far more secure than that!

The Lord Jesus Christ is the foundation of the church. Simon Peter just happened to be the one who gave a sterling

confession of the truth about Jesus. Jesus had asked what they
(the disciples) had to say about him, and Simon Peter
answered, 'You are the Christ, the Son of the living God' (v.
16).

The name Peter comes from the Greek word *'petros'* and
means 'little rock'. When Peter uttered this glowing testimony
of faith, the Lord Jesus responded by using Peter's name in a
play on words. He literally said, 'You are Peter (*petros* — little
rock), but I am going to build my church on this rock (*petra* —
big rock).' In other words, Peter, the little rock, had given
expression to something that was truly big, something so
gigantic, massive and firm that the church could be built upon
it: the truth about the Lord Jesus Christ.

Jesus himself is, then, the foundation of the church. But
does this fact guarantee the ultimate triumph of the church?
Anyone who raises such a question only gives evidence that he
knows very little about the Lord Jesus. This was no ordinary
man, but God himself in human flesh. And God is unlimited
in power.

The Lord Jesus gave indisputable evidence that he is
himself the omnipotent God in human flesh when he arose
from the grave. When he died on the cross all the fiends of hell
must have danced in glee because they thought they had finally
prevailed against the plan of God to build the church. But their
glee was short-lived. When Jesus arose, he showed once and
for all that he has supreme authority over death, hell and the
grave.

This is the one who said, 'I will build my church.' In spite
of false doctrine, in spite of hypocrisy, in spite of apathetic
Christians, in spite of all the machinations of hell, Jesus Christ
is going to build his church. The other promises we have
looked at have had conditions attached, but here is a promise
that is unconditional. Jesus Christ is going to build his church,
come what may.

The proper response

What should our response be to all of this? First, if the church is ultimately going to triumph over all, the most pressing piece of business is to make sure we are part of that church. There is good news for all those who are not yet part of his church: flee to Jesus Christ, repent of your sins, trust him as your Lord and Saviour, commit yourself to live for him and you will be included in his church.

Secondly, if we are already part of this glorious church, we need to be loving it and living for it. Understand this: if you are not doing your best for the church of Jesus Christ, you are being used by Satan to destroy it. There is no middle ground here. May God help us to see it and to say with Timothy Dwight:

> I love thy church, O God;
> Her walls before thee stand,
> Dear as the apple of thine eye,
> And graven on thy hand.
> For her my tears shall fall;
> For her my prayers ascend;
> To her my cares and toils be given
> Till toils and cares shall end.

19.
The promise of forgiveness for the Christian who sins

1 John 1:9

The Greek word *'koinonia'*, which is usually translated in our English Bibles as 'fellowship', was a favourite expression among the Greeks for the marital relationship. In other words, it was most commonly used to describe the most intimate bond between human beings. In his first epistle John takes that word for closeness and intimacy and applies it to the Christian's relationship to God (1 John 1:3). The Christian is one who is in fellowship with God. He knows God in an intimate sort of way.

Have you, child of God, stopped to reflect on that recently? Have you considered what a privilege, what an awesome wonder it is to know God personally and intimately?

We live in a day in which people are awed by the trivial and the unimportant. Sporting feats, for instance, are constantly proclaimed as 'awesome'. But such things are insignificant compared with what I am talking about. The Christian is one who is in fellowship with God! Stop, Christian, and think about it until your heart is filled with rejoicing. The eternal God who made all things, the God who knows all things, the God who has power over all things — this is the one with whom you are in fellowship! There is no higher human privilege than this. The richest are not rich if they miss out on this. The wisest are not wise if they miss out on this. The most successful are not successful if they miss this.

The disrupting effect of sin

The promise John makes in our text is addressed to those who have been blessed with this indescribable privilege. It deals with the one thing that can hamper and disrupt this privilege of fellowship with God — sin.

It is very important that we understand that sin can never destroy the Christian's relationship with God. Nothing can ever destroy that. As we have noted, the one who truly knows God is eternally secure.

But we must be careful not to distort this teaching about the believer's security. Some take it to mean a person can know Christ and yet live any way he or she wants. The apostle John shows the folly of such thinking right here in this first chapter of this epistle. He says, 'If we say that we have fellowship with him, and walk in darkness, we lie and do not practise the truth' (v. 6).

Have you ever tried to put one foot in a boat and keep the other foot planted on the bank? It is impossible. And it is equally impossible for someone to know Christ and yet to live continually in sin. John says the one who thinks he can do 'the splits', so to speak, in terms of the Christian walk is not really a child of God at all.

David Jackman states the point powerfully: 'A person who persists in sin cannot be in touch with God. The two states are mutually exclusive. You might just as well live in a coal pit and claim that you are developing a sun tan!'[1]

But having said all that, I must go on to say it is still possible for the Christian to commit acts of sin. He cannot continually live in sin, but he can at any given moment fall into sin. John also makes this clear by saying, 'If we say that we have no sin, we deceive ourselves, and the truth is not in us' (v. 8). Even though the Christian is forgiven of his sin and brought into that glorious state of fellowship with God, sin still resides in his nature (v. 10) and can and does break out in his conduct from time to time.

There is ample proof of this in the lives of the greatest heroes of the faith. Look at Noah, Abraham, Isaac, Moses, David and Simon Peter. They were all remarkable men of God, and yet the Bible tells us about sin in their lives. If they were not able to live without sin, we may rest assured we shall fall far short of perfection ourselves.

So the Christian does not live continually in sin, but he does commit sin from time to time. When the Christian does fall into sin it always takes a toll on his relationship with God. It disturbs his fellowship with God. It grieves the Lord and causes him to withdraw from the believer. It erects a barrier between the believer and God. It often causes the believer to lose his assurance of salvation and brings him under the chastising hand of God.

When one partner in a marriage does something to offend the other, their closeness is damaged. So it is when the Christian sins. An act of sin does not mean the Christian has lost his relationship with God any more than a quarrel between husband and wife means they cease to be married. But sin does damage. It blocks the channel of fellowship between the believer and God.

Is this channel blocked between us and God at this very moment? Are we seeing little of the power and blessing of God upon the church today because many of us have debris in the channel?

The restoring power of confession

Any act of sin is to the Christian like a stone in his shoe. He just cannot be comfortable as long as it remains there. So how does he get the stone out? This promise also deals with the one thing that gets the sin out and restores fellowship between the believer and God, and that is confession.

Confession does not sound very much to many professing Christians. Some seem to make it nothing more than casually shrugging it off with a remark such as 'Well, nobody's perfect.' Others make it a matter of going to an altar, breezily saying, 'Lord, forgive me of all my sins,' and bouncing up to do the same thing again.

We may be sure there is much more to it than that. It literally means to agree with God about our sin. It sounds simple enough, doesn't it? But it is not simple. What does it mean to agree with God?

It means we see sin with his eyes; we understand how heinous and vile it is.

It means we call sin by its right name (e.g., adultery instead of 'having an affair').

It means we feel deep grief that we could be so ungrateful to the God who loved us and saved us as to break his commandments.

It means we solemnly resolve to do whatever is necessary to keep from repeating the sin.

It means we demonstrate by word and by life that we have left this sin behind.

It means we make restitution to anyone who has been harmed by our sin.

What happens when we agree with God about our sin? He forgives us! He wipes the slate clean! We may not feel as if he has forgiven us, but it is not a matter of feeling. We have his promise that he will forgive us if we sincerely confess.

How do we know he will do it? John answers by saying God is 'faithful and just'. His faithfulness means he is dependable. If he says he will do something, we can depend on him to do it.

His justice means, if I may so state it, that he has to forgive our sins. Why? Because on the cross Jesus fully paid the debt for our sins — not just the sins we committed before our salvation but even those sins we commit as Christians. If God has already punished those sins in Christ, and if I as a Christian come to him pleading for forgiveness, God's justice demands that he forgive me. God cannot punish me for what he has already punished Christ for and still be just. So when I come to him in true confession, he forgives me. This is the reason John says the blood of Jesus goes on cleansing us from our sin (v. 7).

> When Satan tempts me to despair,
> And tells me of the guilt within,
> Upward I look, and see him there
> Who made an end of all my sin.
> Because the sinless Saviour died,
> My sinful soul is counted free;
> For God, the just, is satisfied
> To look on him and pardon me.

The urgent need for examination

That brings us to consider a final aspect of this promise. It suggests the one thing we most urgently need to do is conduct an examination.

There are *sins of commission* that we need to look for. We are guilty of sins of commission when we do something the

Lord tells us not to do. Lying, gossiping, stealing, adultery —
these are, along with a host of others, things the Lord has
strictly forbidden.

Then there are *sins of omission*. We are guilty of these sins
when we fail to do what the Lord has commanded us to do. If
we fail to attend church and fail to truly worship God when we
get there, we have sinned. If we fail to pray, we are guilty of
a sin of omission. If we fail to forgive someone, we have
omitted something God has commanded. There is no shortage
of omissions in the lives of most of us.

And there are *sins of the disposition*. Some of us think as
long as we do not actually commit the overt act we are all
right, but we allow sinful thoughts into our minds and allow
them to shape our attitudes. Bitterness, anger, envy and hatred
are all sins of disposition. With most sins of the disposition we
usually get a great deal of satisfaction because we think we are
hurting someone else. But we are really only hurting
ourselves.

Child of God, you have been blessed with the highest
privilege any human being can ever have: fellowship with
God. Only sin can keep you from enjoying that fellowship.
Examine yourself. Do not let sin rob you of the blessing of God
and the enjoyment of your salvation. If you are doing something wrong, confess it and stop it. If you are failing to do
something right, confess your failure and start doing it. If you
are nurturing a sour disposition, confess it and sweeten it.

When Christians sin they do a lot of damage. They not only
disrupt their fellowship with God, but they also disturb their
own inner peace. And they cause those who are not Christians
to think there is nothing to Christianity and to feel secure in
their unbelief. There is so much at stake here — too much for
us to go another minute without examining our hearts and
confessing our sins.

20.
The promise of healing for the land

2 Chronicles 7:12-14

The words of the text are God's answer to Solomon's prayer. In the course of dedicating Israel's new temple to the Lord, Solomon had earnestly sought the Lord to look with favour upon the temple and upon the people of the nation.

He realized, of course, that the gleaming new temple was not sufficient to secure God's favour. The people had to walk with God and obey his commandments. And Solomon also knew the sinful inclinations of his people. When, if the people sinned against God, would he ever look with favour upon them again? That was the question surging through his mind as he prayed. The last part of his prayer is filled with the words 'if' and 'then' (2 Chron. 6:22-39). Here is what he was asking: 'if' the people sinned, fell under God's judgement and turned back to the Lord, would the Lord 'then' hear, forgive and restore them?

Our text reveals that the Lord answered Solomon's prayer that night with an 'if' and a 'then' of his own. He assured Solomon that if his people would turn from their sins he would then hear them, forgive them and heal their land.

A definite need

It is the last part of this promise — the healing of the land — that so many Christians can identify with these days. There are many nations today that are in desperate need of healing.

I can testify to the need of my own country, the United States. Recent studies show astounding moral and spiritual decline. Crime soars. Families disintegrate. Drug usage abounds. The teen suicide rate climbs steadily. Sexual immorality rages. Child abuse flows along unabated. The condition of the nation has become such a matter of grave concern that one newspaper columnist sombrely pronounces 'our pulse weak, respiration laboured, temperature lethally elevated, and ... blood pressure low'. And he goes on to add: 'For this sick patient, day is almost done.'[1]

One of the few encouraging reasons for hope in the USA is that it is virtually impossible to find anyone who will dispute that the patient is indeed dreadfully sick. There is, mind you, precious little agreement on what can be done to restore her heath, but almost everyone agrees the nation needs heroic medical treatment. Sadly, what is true of the United States is also found in other nations as well.

A definite link

It is this matter of restoring nations to health that leads me to say there is a definite link between the spiritual health of God's people and the health of their nations.

We need to be careful at this point. Some take what the Scriptures have to say about the nation of Israel in the Old Testament and apply it in a national sense today, but that is a mistake. No nation today occupies the same position that Israel did. The nation of Israel was in a special covenant relationship with God, and there is now no national counterpart to that. The modern-day parallel of Old Testament Israel is the church of Christ, as the apostle Paul makes clear in Romans 2:28-29 and Galatians 3:29.

This promise of healing for the land is probably most properly applied, therefore, to the healing of sick churches. But having said that, I must go on to say that the health of Christians and the health of their nation are still inextricably woven together. Jesus says his followers are the salt of the earth (Matt. 5:13). Salt is a preservative. Rub it into meat and it will keep the meat from decaying. In like fashion, Christians are to have a godly influence on their society. Their presence should retard moral decay in their society. R. V. G. Tasker says Jesus' disciples are '... to be a moral disinfectant in a world where moral standards are low, constantly changing, or non-existent'.[2]

But if the salt loses its saltiness — a very real possibility according to Jesus (Matt. 5:13) — there is nothing to retard the moral decay of society. How does salt lose its saltiness? John R.W. Stott writes, 'Now, strictly speaking, salt can never lose its saltiness ... sodium chloride is a very stable chemical compound, which is resistant to nearly every attack. Nevertheless, it can become contaminated by mixture with impurities, and then it becomes useless, even dangerous.' He then makes this application: 'If Christians become assimilated to non-Christians and contaminated by the world, they lose their influence.'[3]

Do we have here the explanation for the moral degradation we see in so many countries? I think we do. Christians have become contaminated with their societies and, therefore, have lost their capacity to retard their decay and to influence them for God. The greatest tragedy is not that there is so much iniquity sweeping across so many nations today. It is especially tragic that these nations can be the way they are in view of the fact that so many of their citizens profess to be Christians. How can so many profess to be Christians and not have more of a positive influence? The answer is that many who profess Christ do not truly know him and many who do know him have become contaminated salt.

A call to renewal

If this is true, it forces us to say the most urgent need of our day is for God's people to address their own spiritual condition.

How we Christians need to recognize this! We so easily get caught up in bemoaning the conditions of our day and in pointing fingers of condemnation at wicked people and their wicked ways. But if the sequence unfolded above is true, it means God's finger is pointed squarely at his own people. If our nations are desperately ill with wickedness it is because we have not been salty salt.

We also need urgently to recognize what we must do to get the saltiness back. We are mistaken if we think any nation can be healed by political action. Christians are entitled, of course, to exercise the same rights of citizenship as anyone else, but, in the final analysis, the only way to heal sick lands is for us as Christians to get our saltiness back. How are we to do that? God's Word gives a clear and unvarnished answer. We are to humble ourselves, pray, seek God's face and turn from our wicked ways.

We are to *humble ourselves* because we have so often been proud and have taken for granted that there is nothing lacking in our walk with the Lord. Like the church of Laodicea we have often said, 'I am rich, have become wealthy, and have need of nothing' (Rev. 3:17).

We need to *pray* because prayer is the way we talk to God. And we do need to talk to him! He is the one we have offended. He has called us to be his salty people and he is offended with our lack of saltiness and with our coldness, our casualness and our carelessness. There is no way for us to get our saltiness back without speaking to the God we have offended.

We need to *seek God's face*. This means we must realize we need God. We are nothing without him! We need his blessings upon our lives, upon our families, upon our churches and upon our nation, or we shall make a mess out of each.

We need to *turn from our wicked ways*. Have we become
contaminated with the thinking and doing of the world? Then
we need to put these things away. Here is where so many of us
fail. We are willing to admit we have failed to be God's salty
people and we are willing to ask God to forgive us for failing,
but we have no intention of forsaking our sins. We want God
to forgive us but we want to carry on using our foul language,
watching our filthy TV programmes, disregarding the Lord's
Day, nursing resentment in our hearts towards our brothers
and sisters in Christ, and on and on and on. May God help us
to see the price we are paying for our refusal to turn from our
sins! There will be no return to saltiness without turning from
our sins and there will be no healing for our nations without our
return to saltiness.

These four steps to saltiness are steps we as individuals
must take. A church cannot repent. A nation cannot repent. But
individuals can. What is a church except a collection of
individuals? What is a nation except the sum of its individuals?
So often we are guilty of looking at the sickness of our land and
saying, 'Yes, it's terrible, but what can one person do?' The
answer is that one Christian can make sure he is as salty as he
can possibly be.

We have astounding historical precedents to cheer us in this
matter of returning to saltiness. When God's people have
taken these four steps, God has indeed healed whole nations.

The greatest example is England during the ministries of
George Whitefield and John and Charles Wesley. J. R. Green,
in *A Short History of the English People,* says of those days:
'A religious revival burst forth ... which changed in a few
years the whole temper of English society. The Church was
restored to life and activity. Religion carried to the hearts of the
people a fresh spirit of moral zeal, while it purified our
literature, infused clemency and wisdom into our penal laws,
abolished the slave trade, and gave the first impulse to popular
education.'[4]

All of that from God's people getting their saltiness back? Yes! And it can happen again in our own day and age. Thank God, nations can be healed, but healing will come only if God's people become deeply concerned about their spiritual condition and take prompt and serious action.

The promise God gave to Solomon regarding the healing of the land inevitably causes us to think of the Lord Jesus Christ. God had promised to build a permanent house for Solomon's father David (2 Sam. 7:16). That promise was to be fulfilled by Christ. Only he could secure the eternal throne God promised David. David's descendants, including Solomon, proved to be unfaithful to God. Their unfaithfulness was such that God finally punished them by sending them away into captivity in Babylon, and it appeared that God's promise of a permanent throne for David would come to nought. But it didn't. David had a greater Son, the Lord Jesus Christ, and he now reigns over a new Israel, composed of all those whom he has redeemed from sin, and that reign will never end.

One of the dimensions of God's promise to Solomon, then, was that he would not prove unfaithful even if his people proved unfaithful. S. G. DeGraaf says of the unfaithfulness of Solomon and his people, 'Over against their unfaithfulness, the faithfulness of the Lord's grace in the eternal sovereign rule of the Christ shines all the more brilliantly.'[5]

21.
A promise for tearful sowers

Psalm 126

This psalm is one of fifteen designated as 'A Song of Ascents' (Ps. 120-134). These songs were sung by pilgrims as they drew near to Jerusalem for the various religious festivals. They probably derived their name from two sources. First, pilgrims literally had to 'ascend' to go to Jerusalem because it was situated in a mountainous region (Ps. 125:1-2). Secondly, the pilgrims undoubtedly found their spirits ascending as they drew near the city and it was, therefore, fitting for them to express this by singing.

The psalm before us falls quite naturally into three parts. In verses 1-3 the psalmist speaks to his fellow-worshippers. In verse 4 he speaks to God. In verses 5-6 the Lord answers the psalmist.

Looking back to a remarkable time

The words of the psalmist to his fellow-worshippers deal with a remarkable episode in their history. The psalmist characterizes this as a time 'when the Lord brought back the captivity of Zion' (v. 1).

Most of the psalms were written during the reign of King David, but these opening words would seem to refer to something that occurred many centuries after David's time, namely, the release of the Jews from their years of captivity in Babylon. The fact that most of the psalms were written during David's time does not preclude later songs being added to the collection, and that is probably what happened in this instance.

The Jews underwent a great spiritual renewal while they were there in Babylon. They came to see that their captivity was a result of their sins, and they undoubtedly made a thorough job of repentance during their time in exile.

Then came the good news that they were going to be allowed to return to their homeland. The psalmist describes the torrent of joy that broke out when they received that word. He says first that he and his fellow captives were 'like those who dream' (v. 1). In other words, the news was simply too good to be true.

He proceeds to describe the people laughing and singing (v. 2). Their joy was so great that other nations took note of it and concluded: 'The Lord has done great things for them' (v. 2).

There was no doubt in the psalmist's mind that it was indeed the Lord's doing. He begins the psalm by giving credit to the Lord (v. 1), and he concludes this section by agreeing with what the other nations were saying. He says, as it were, 'Yes, you are right. The Lord has done great things for us.' And then he adds these words: 'whereof we are glad' (v. 3).

The psalmist's description of this release from captivity is a wonderful and graphic description of every episode in which God has stepped into the lives of his people to grant them revival or spiritual renewal.

Revival always exceeds our expectations. Revival always opens the floodgates of joy. Revival always leaves a profound impression on those around the people of God.

Looking at present deterioration

But from this joyous note, the psalmist moves to a sombre
note. His reliving of the glory of their release from captivity
suddenly causes him to realize that some slippage has taken
place. In other words, the people are not now as close to God
as they were when they were released from captivity. No, they
had not gone back to the worship of idols (the captivity broke
them of that once and for all), but they had somehow or other
grown complacent about the things of the Lord.

To get a true picture of what happened with these people
after they returned to their land, one has only to read the
prophecies of Malachi and Haggai. For instance, Malachi talks
about the people keeping up the round of religious activities
without any sense of enthusiasm (Mal. 1:13). And Haggai
talks about the people being so occupied with their own
business that they had little interest in the house of the Lord
(Hag. 1:4).

We do not know just where the writer of Psalm 126 fits into
the sequence of events that followed the release from captivity, but he had evidently seen enough to know that the
euphoria of the release had faded and spiritual deterioration
had set in.

Crying for a return to vitality

So we find him praying in verse 4: 'Bring back our captivity,
O Lord, as the streams in the south.' In other words, he was
asking God to do for him and his people something akin to
what he had done when they were released from captivity. He
is saying, 'Turn us back, O Lord, to that time.'

The people's spiritual condition at that time reminded him
of the southern region of their land. Drought always dried up
the streams in that area, but then the rains would come and

those dry stream-beds would be filled with torrents of water. With that picture in his mind, the psalmist was, therefore, asking God to do in the spiritual realm what he did for that southern area. He was asking for a copious outpouring of God's power and grace, one that would take away their dryness and cause them to rejoice again.

With all that in place, we are able finally to look at the promise in verses 5 and 6. In those verses, the Lord speaks to the psalmist regarding the request he has made. The Lord essentially says, 'Do you want what you had when you were released from captivity? Do you want a spiritual flood to relieve your dryness and barrenness? Then here is what you must do — you must sow in tears. If you will sow in tears, I promise that you will reap in joy.'

What was the Lord saying to this psalmist? He was calling upon him and all his people to truly repent of their sins, and then the flood of blessing would come.

We have noted that the people of God repented during their years of captivity in Babylon, and that repentance was as inextricably connected to their release and to the joy that sprang from it as the sowing of a farmer is connected to his reaping.

Now if they wanted to reap that same crop of joy and vibrancy, they would have to sow the same seeds. And if they were unwilling to sow those same seeds, they would have nothing to look forward to except continued spiritual dryness and lethargy.

Applying the truth to our own lives

These words ought to make certain truths very clear and obvious to us. First, if we want an explanation for spiritual decline, we have to look no further than the sins we have allowed to invade our lives.

Another truth that gleams at us from these verses is that sin is a very serious thing and it has to be treated as such. If we want to reap the crop of spiritual renewal and vitality, we must sow 'in tears'.

A casual study of the great revivals of the past will quickly reveal certain outstanding characteristics. In such times the people of God became keenly conscious of the holiness of God and of the extreme preciousness of the gospel. These truths invariably made each sin seem like a sharp stick in the eye, and the people of God could get no peace until they engaged in a thorough, profound work of repentance.

What is a thorough work of repentance? It is one that stops excusing sins, calls them by their right names and turns from them with a true sorrow. In such times of repentance, the Christian is amazed that he could ever allow into his life things that grieve the God to whom he owes so much.

Such repentance is always painful but, thank God, when it has done its work the joy comes just as the promise says: 'Those who sow in tears shall reap in joy.' Those who have studied revivals invariably make mention of the joy that comes to the people of God through repentance. There is nothing quite like it. It is the joy of walking in close communion with God, feeling his presence, knowing his approval. Revival may be likened to the heavenly Father scooping his child up into his arms to embrace him and communicate to him the deep love he has for him. Oh, the joy of that!

Verse 6 shows us another dimension of spiritual renewal. The child of God who tearfully sows the seeds of repentance over the sin in his own life will receive a bag of seed for sowing. And the promise is given that the sowing of these seeds will lead to a bountiful harvest. The result of his sowing will be a great number of 'sheaves' (bundles of grain). What are we to understand by this? Simply this — when the child of God experiences spiritual renewal the Lord will use him or her in sowing the seed of the gospel to others.

What greater incentive could we possibly have to seek personal renewal? Our brokenness not only brings the joy of revival, but also leads to the joy of seeing others come to the saving knowledge of our Lord and Saviour. The history of revival again bears this out. The most fruitful times of evangelism in the church have been those times when the people of God were first broken in repentance over their own sins.

The words of this psalm were written by a man who had a keen memory of past blessings and that memory caused him to lament the spiritual condition of his people. Keen memory of blessings always has this effect. And no Christian can have a keen memory of blessings without thinking first and foremost of the Christ who purchased his salvation on Calvary's cross. The more we bathe ourselves in that atoning death on our behalf, the more we shall be driven to lament our own spiritual condition. Calvary's light always exposes coldness of heart, carelessness about sin and casualness about duties. Gazing long at the cross will finally force us to say in admiration and awe:

Died he for me, who caused his pain?
For me, who him to death pursued?
Amazing love! How can it be,
That thou, my God, shouldst die for me?

The keen memory of Calvary's cross is always the first step towards sowing in tears and reaping in joy.

22.
The promise of renewed strength

Isaiah 40:27-31

The people to whom this promise was originally addressed were about to enter a very difficult period in their lives. They had been living for a prolonged period in flagrant rebellion against God. God had patiently sent prophet after prophet to call them back to himself, but they had refused to heed.

There is an end to the patience of God, and he was about to send them off into captivity in far-away Babylon. Babylon was a strength-sapping place. There the people of Judah would feel the full force of depleted strength. One of the psalms expresses the devastation the people felt when this captivity took place:

By the rivers of Babylon,
There we sat down, yea, we wept
When we remembered Zion.
We hung our harps
Upon the willows in the midst of it.
For there those who carried us away captive required of
us a song,
And those who plundered us required of us mirth,
Saying, 'Sing us one of the songs of Zion!'
(Ps. 137:1-4).

The prophet Isaiah ministered before this sad captivity took place, but he could see it coming and he knew exactly what his people would be saying once they were there: 'My way is hidden from the Lord, and my just claim is passed over by my God' (v. 27). In other words, the people of Judah would feel as if God had totally cast them off, that there was no purpose in going on — in fact that they were unable to go on!

Isaiah makes it clear that this would be the sentiment of all those in captivity. We usually think young people are able to adapt quickly to massive changes and resilient enough to bounce back from life's hardships, but as Isaiah casts his gaze over the coming captivity, he sees even the young fainting and hears the young men sighing under the crushing burden (v. 30).

But even when God judges his people, he does not forget to be gracious. So before they were taken captive, he gave them some promises to fortify them. Matthew Henry explains it like this: 'Before God sent his people into captivity he furnished them with precious promises for their support and comfort in their trouble; and we may well imagine of what great use to them the glorious, gracious, light of this prophecy was, in that cloudy and dark day, and how much it helped to dry up their tears by the rivers of Babylon.'[1]

One of those promises is found in our text: 'Those who wait on the Lord shall renew their strength...' (v. 31). What does it mean to wait on the Lord? It means not to give up on God but to continue believing he will do what he has promised to do even though our circumstances seem to dictate otherwise. It means living on the basis of the Word of God when everything appears to contradict it.

Before God sent his people away into captivity, he gave them the distinct promise that he would eventually bring them back into their homeland. He says,

Behold, the Lord God shall come with a strong hand,
And his arm shall rule for him;

Behold, his reward is with him
And his work before him.
He will feed his flock like a shepherd;
He will gather the lambs with his arm,
And carry them in his bosom,
And gently lead those who are with young

(vv. 10-11).

So there they are in the land of Babylon, and their situation is so difficult and trying that they begin to jump to the conclusion that God has abandoned them (v. 27). Their strength is sapped. Their hope is gone. All appears to be lost.

But all is not lost. Isaiah's word comes to them to say, 'The way for you to cope with Babylon is to look beyond Babylon to that time when our nation will be restored to her land.' Cope with the evil present by looking towards a glorious future! Is there any sense in that? Yes! We know from experience that we can put up with almost anything if we know it is temporary!

It sounds easy enough to wait on the Lord. But it is not easy. Someone over here is saying, 'You tell us to wait on the Lord, but how do we know he cares about us?' Isaiah says even though God has judged them he still cares for them as a shepherd cares for his flock (v. 11).

But someone over there cries, 'Maybe God wants to fulfil his promise to restore us to our land, but he won't be able to do so.' Isaiah says, 'Let me tell you about the limitless power of our God.' And then he plunges into a lengthy description of the power and majesty of God. He is the one who measures the great bodies of water by holding them in his hand and weighs the towering mountains on a balance (v. 12). All the nations of the earth are nothing more than drops in a bucket or specks of dust before his eyes (v. 15). Even the whole earth itself is like a small circle to him and all the inhabitants of it are like so many small grasshoppers (v. 22).

We are impressed by the vastness of the heavens. Consider this: God is the one who created all these things. He has set all the heavenly bodies in their places, he knows all their names and he keeps them doing what he created them to do (v. 26).

Isaiah, as it were, takes the biggest things he can think of and holds them up against God. But the oceans, the mountains, the nations, the earth itself and all its inhabitants, and even the vast realm of space, are all as nothing when compared with the greatness of God. May God help us to get just a glimpse of this God who far surpasses and transcends the greatest things we can think of!

It should be evident from all this that the waiting Isaiah called for was no mere passive resignation to the circumstances. It required a great deal of actively reminding oneself of who God is. And that led, in turn, to an active and eager expectation of what he was going to do.

Isaiah further assures the people that waiting on the Lord to fulfil his promise to them would have a most salutary effect upon them. They would soar as eagles. They would run and not be weary. They would walk and not faint.

The soaring as eagles may indicate that they would be able to rise above the despondency and depression of their circumstances and find communion with God in the midst of them. They would then be able to meet the demands placed upon them by life in Babylon. If their circumstances there required them to run briskly in discharging responsibility they would be able to do it. If their circumstances became humdrum and monotonous and life dragged along, they would be able to walk through it. The key to their situation was to trust the Lord's promise. That would cause their spirits to soar and would enable them to cope with their circumstances.

All of this is filled with meaning and relevance for God's people today. We know something of Babylon today. No, most Christians have not been rudely plucked from their homes and hurled into a far-away land. But we do not need to pack up and move to be in Babylon. It has a way of coming to us. Difficult, trying circumstances that make God seem distant and going forward seem impossible mean Babylon has come to us.

What are we to do about it all? The word of Isaiah comes hurtling over the centuries to tell us the answer is the same for us as it was for those Jewish captives in that far-away time — Wait! Wait on the Lord!

We have a glorious message in the Word of God. It is a message about the eternal Son of God stepping into human history as a man, living in perfect obedience to God's law and going to a Roman cross to lay down his life for our sins. It is a message about him rising from the dead and ascending to the right hand of the Father to make intercession for us. It is a message about his sufficiency for us each and every day. It is a message about his coming again to receive us unto himself.

This message about Christ is not merely a message we believe for our salvation before we move on to other things. It is a message for us to feed upon each day. The apostle Paul says, 'As you have therefore received Christ Jesus the Lord, so walk in him, rooted and built up in him and established in the faith, as you have been taught, abounding in it with thanksgiving' (Col. 2:6-7).

This is a strength-giving message. As we talk to it, and allow it to talk to us, we find our doubts, our weariness, our despondency draining away and strength flowing in. Indeed, as we realize the glory of it all, we even find ourselves soaring — soaring in worship that God would be gracious enough to provide such an astounding salvation for us. And as we soar in worship, we find ourselves soaring over our circumstances, and that will enable us then to run in the discharge of responsibility and to unfaintingly walk when life is humdrum and monotonous.

Or, if we may select just one of Isaiah's metaphors, we may say our ability to run with endurance in life's race comes from 'looking unto Jesus, the author and finisher of our faith' (Heb. 12:2).

Our choice in our modern-day Babylon is this — we can hang our harps on her trees and weep, or we can hang our hearts on Calvary's tree, worship God for what he has done in Christ and trustingly wait for him to fulfil all he has promised to do. Strength comes from the latter.

23.
The golden promise

Romans 8:28

Few words have provoked a wider range of reactions than those which we find in this verse. Some bristle when they read it. They immediately think of circumstances that have gone sour, and they can find no way to reconcile them with the good promised in this verse.

Others, however, embrace this verse with profound love and appreciation. It gives them untold peace and comfort in the hour of trial. They readily agree with the Puritan Thomas Brooks, who called it 'that golden promise'. They see that this promise really explains more of the mysteries of this life than any other.

There is no debate that life is mystifying. All kinds of afflictions and trials beset us here. Paul says all of creation is racked with pain (8:22-23) as it waits expectantly for a better future. We Christians are caught up in the sufferings of this world, but we have as a resource the Holy Spirit who helps us in our weakness (8:26). Even with his help, Christians still suffer. How are we to explain the suffering that befalls us? That is where this promise comes in.

A restriction

There are several things for us to note about this promise. First, it quite obviously contains a restriction. It does not apply to all people without exception. Paul explicitly limits it to those who love God and to those who are 'the called according to his purpose'.

In this sentimental age, many are quick to assume that they love God and, therefore, qualify for this promise. But the message of the Bible is that love to God is not natural to us. We come into this world with a nature that is opposed to God (Rom. 8:7).

How, then, does anyone come to love God? The only way anyone can love God is through God graciously working in his or her heart to remove the hostility that is there and create a whole new disposition.

Those who love God are the ones he has 'called' unto himself. When God changes the disposition of the heart, he also calls the sinner into a saving relationship with himself with a call that is effectual and powerful.

Here we have the explanation for why any of us love God. God loved us first and called us to himself. The apostle John declares: 'We love him because he first loved us' (1 John 4:19).

No one would ever love God unless God had first loved him. We are face to face here with the fact that our salvation is due solely to the grace of God. We can do nothing to earn it or deserve it. It happens as the God who loved us before time began calls us to himself in the midst of time. The Christian, then, is one who has, to use the words of the apostle Paul, been 'apprehended' (Phil. 3:12,13). God stepped into the life of each Christian and so interrupted and disrupted that person's life that he or she came to faith in Jesus Christ.

No one is saved who has not been confronted and convicted by God, or to use Paul's expression, 'called' by God. The Christian says with the poet:

I hear thy welcome voice
That calls me, Lord, to thee,
For cleansing in thy precious blood
That flowed on Calvary.

A purpose

With this restriction in place, we are able to move to another consideration — that is, God's overriding purpose for his people.

Paul refers to those who are the called according to God's purpose. It was God's purpose to call his people unto himself (our salvation is not a haphazard thing, but was planned by God before the world began), and he purposed to call us unto himself that he might achieve another purpose. That purpose is that we might be 'conformed to the image of his Son' (v. 29).

God wants us to progressively and increasingly reflect the glory of his Son from the time we are called by God until the time he finally takes us home. At that time he will complete the process so that we shall then perfectly reflect the glory of Christ for ever. Only if we understand God's purpose for us can we truly comprehend the provision or the heart of the promise.

In keeping with his goal to conform us to the image of Christ, our God works all things together for good. The 'good' for which God works all things together is his purpose to conform us to the image of Christ — that is, to make us Christlike.

The reason why so many have trouble accepting this promise is that they insist on interpreting the good to mean whatever makes their lives more pleasant and comfortable. When any kind of difficulty arises, they find themselves wondering how such a thing could possibly be for their good.

But the good God has in mind is not our comfort but our conformity to Christ. And to achieve that conformity he often has to send us circumstances that run counter to our comfort. The promise does not assert that everything God sends our way will be good, but rather that God uses even those things that are not good to produce that conformity that he desires.

A comprehensiveness

That brings us to consider the extent of this promise. It quite literally comprehends 'all things'. The picture here is of God gathering up all the diverse strands of our existence and moulding them together into a unified whole.

We have no trouble, of course, in seeing how God can use the good things of this life to bring about good, but we are staggered by the thought of God using evil things to attain a good end.

The classic example of this truth comes from the life of Joseph. He had been treated in cruel fashion by his brothers, sold by them into slavery in Egypt. There, through the providence of God, he had risen to a position of great authority, second only to Pharaoh. Here is how Joseph looked on the evil his brothers had done in selling him into slavery: 'But as for you, you meant evil against me; but God meant it for good, in order to bring it about as it is this day, to save many people alive' (Gen. 50:20).

An illustration of this principle of bringing good out of evil is a doctor performing surgery. The surgery involves pain and suffering. But no one accuses the doctor of being cruel because of the pain he induces through the surgery. Everyone recognizes that the doctor's purpose in bringing about the immediate pain of his patient is so that he might ultimately bring about good for that patient.

A certainty

There is one more thing for us to notice about this promise and that is the certainty of it. Did you notice how the apostle begins this verse? He says, 'We know...' We might have preferred 'We hope...', or 'We desire...', or 'We pray...', or even 'We think...' But instead he says, 'We know...' Paul was not indulging in hyperbole — intentional overstatement for the purpose of emphasis. No, this is his sober, considered conviction and he assumes that all Christians join him in it.

How can we share his confidence? By looking at the scriptures which teach the same thing as this promise. Scripture after scripture affirms the same truth that this promise affirms. This is how Paul was able to write these words. He was steeped in the Old Testament where God's people were called 'the apple of his eye' (Deut. 32:10; Zech. 2:8).

Paul knew, for instance, the words of Proverbs 3:6: 'In all your ways acknowledge him, and he shall direct your paths.' That verse affirms the same principle: God is guiding and controlling all the circumstances of his people.

Psalm 91:11 states: 'For he shall give his angels charge over you, to keep you in all your ways.' Again, it is the same teaching as we have in our text.

Also in the Scriptures Paul saw the examples of great men like Jacob, Job, David and the man I have already mentioned, Joseph. How does one explain all that happened in the lives of these men? Paul could explain it only in terms of God overruling their circumstances and bringing about good, so he says, 'We know...'

Then there were Paul's own experiences. In his second letter to the Corinthians, he includes a long list of his sufferings. These are not good things. He mentions imprisonments, beatings, shipwrecks and robberies (2 Cor. 11:23-33). But while these things were not good in themselves, they brought about good. Through them he was increasingly moulded into conformity to Christ, and that conformity made him the mighty apostle that led multitudes to the saving knowledge of Christ.

We can rest assured that God is doing the same thing in each of his children. No, he is not making us into mighty apostles, as in Paul's case, but in all our circumstances, he is working for our conformity to Christ and is using that to further his kingdom.

We are not able, of course, to see all that in this life. We know it is happening because we have his word regarding it. But we are unable to say with precision how this or that particular evil circumstance can be part of God's plan to bring about our good.

It is not necessary for us to understand it all. It is enough that we know that we have a loving heavenly Father who is committed to our best interests. When we cannot trace his hand, we can trust his heart. Knowing this, we are able to join the poet in gladly affirming:

The things that happen unto me
Are not by chance, I know,
But because my Father's wisdom
Has willed to have it so.
For the 'furtherance of the gospel'
As a part of his great plan,
God can use our disappointments
And the weaknesses of man.

24.
The promise of God's vindication of the righteous

Malachi 3:16 - 4:3

The Bible says there are only two classes of people in this world: those who are saved and those who are not. Or, to use other terms, there are the righteous and the wicked, the children of God and the children of the world, believers and unbelievers, the godly and the ungodly.

This is not popular teaching. Ours is a day in which many prefer to believe there is only one class — children of God — and all are automatically in that class.

Others see the fallacy in that, but they still cannot abide the idea of there being only two classes. They argue, therefore, that there are really three classes: the saved, the lost and those who are really saved but live all their lives as if they were lost.

No matter how attractive and appealing these other options are, the Bible emphatically assures us on page after page and in line after line that there are only two classes — not one, not three, but two.

The righteous described

The prophet Malachi describes for us those who belong to that class we can call the righteous, or the children of God.

1. They fear the Lord

He first says that they fear the Lord (3:16). That means they hold God in highest reverence. We are so constituted that we must reverence something. There must be something in our lives that awes us and moves us to deep allegiance. For some it is money. For others it is sports or pleasure. For still others it is power and prestige. With Christians, it is God. This does not mean they have no place at all for such things as possessions or pleasures; it simply means that such things do not hold the place of supreme allegiance in their lives.

Christians are not, therefore, casual or nonchalant about God. They stand in awe of his person, they submit to his authority and they dread his displeasure. Note that Malachi simply states this as a fact. He does not say the righteous should fear the Lord, but he matter-of-factly observes that they do fear the Lord.

If this is true of the righteous, it is simple logic that the unrighteous do not fear the Lord. The Bible flatly asserts this: 'There is no fear of God before their eyes' (Rom. 3:18). Someone has observed that the essence of ungodliness is to refuse to be afraid of God when there is reason to be afraid.

2. They meet together

Malachi begins, then, with the basic point. The righteous are those who fear God. Then he goes on to note a couple of natural outcomes of this basic ingredient. He says the righteous speak often to one another. This is inevitable. We have often heard it said that birds of a feather flock together. If someone has the fear of God in his heart it is only natural for him to desire to be with others who share that interest. So there is a public dimension to his fear of God. Is it possible to have the fear of

God in our hearts and not have in those same hearts the desire
to be with others who share that fear?

3. They think on his name

Then there is a private dimension to the righteous. He not only
gathers with others like him, but *he also meditates on the
name of God*. He delights in God and enjoys thinking about
him.

It should go without saying that the righteous are blessed of
God. After all, they do reverence him, they meet with his
children and they think upon his name. So it is only natural to
expect them to be blessed by God, and in many ways they are.

A puzzle presented

This brings us, however, to a great dilemma — the fact that the
righteous often do not appear to be different in terms of
blessing from the unrighteous.

This was a real problem for many of Malachi's people.
They could easily look around and see people who made no
pretence of serving God but were getting along much better
than those who were serving God. Some of the people were so
discouraged by this that they were actually saying some
terrible things like, 'Everyone who does evil is good in the
sight of the Lord, and he delights in them' (2:17). And that
sentiment led many of them to ask, 'Where is the God of
justice?' (2:17). Yet another comment they were making was:
'So now we call the proud blessed, for those who do wickedness are raised up; yes, those who tempt God go free' (3:15).

The people of Malachi's time were not the only ones who
struggled with this problem. The psalmist Asaph wrote a

lengthy piece in which he wondered why the wicked pros-
pered while the people of God suffered. At one point he says:

> Behold, these are the ungodly
> Who are always at ease;
> They increase in riches.
> Surely I have cleansed my heart in vain,
> And washed my hands in innocence.
> For all day long I have been plagued,
> And chastened every morning
>
> (Ps. 73:12-14).

Asaph begins this psalm by confessing that he had allowed
this problem to drive him to the very brink of despair. He says,
'My feet had almost stumbled; my steps had nearly slipped'
(v. 1).

Almost every child of God can say the same problem has
caused him or her to stumble or slip at one time or another.
Most of us would have to admit that, in the light of how blessed
the wicked are, we have wondered with Malachi's people if it
is really vain to serve the Lord (3:14).

Even unbelievers themselves are aware of this problem.
When a Christian talks to them about their need for Christ, they
say, 'Look, I'm getting along just as well as you are. Why do
I need Christ?'

A day anticipated

How are we to deal with this dilemma? God has, in his grace,
given certain promises to help us, and some of them are right
here in Malachi's prophecy. Putting them together, we can say
there is a day coming when the difference between the righteous and the wicked will be crystal clear.

The difference between believers and unbelievers may not always be apparent in this life, but, in the words of T. V. Moore, there is coming a 'great day of final adjustment ... in which all seeming anomalies of the present shall be fully explained and wholly removed for ever.'[1]

What day is this great day? It is the day when this life is over and eternity finally dawns. Where will that great day find the people of God? The Lord says it will find them safe with him.

Those of us who have been saved by his grace have not yet begun to understand the greatness of God's love towards his people. The Lord regards us as his precious jewels (3:17), and he tells us that there is a glad day coming when he will gather us unto himself.

In this world, the people of God are regarded as anything but precious jewels. In this world, they are scattered amidst the dirt and mire. They are often treated with disdain and disgust. On that day they will at long last be rewarded and vindicated. Nothing they have ever done for the Lord's honour and glory will be forgotten because God is keeping a 'book of remembrance' (3:16).

It was a common practice among ancient kings to keep such a book. Any subject who rendered a service to the king had his name and what he had done noted in that book, and in due time the king would reward him (Esth. 6:1). God is keeping a book of remembrance in which even the smallest service is noted. When the people of God come together and speak to one another about their God, their slightest whisper of praise is noted and will be rewarded. The Lord Jesus struck this same note when Peter asked what he and the other disciples would receive for following him. Jesus said everyone who follows him 'shall receive a hundredfold' (Matt. 19:29).

The dawning of that glorious eternal day is going to be an occasion of unspeakable joy and praise. Malachi says it will be a day when God's people will 'skip about like calves from the stall' (4:2, NASB).

With a God who regards us as his precious jewels and who rewards even our minutest form of service, why should we worry about the wicked prospering more than Christians in this life?

But what about the wicked? Where will the dawning of that eternal day find them? The Lord has no glowing, wonderful words to say about their future. Quite the contrary. For them, the eternal day will be one of raging fire and they will be like stubble in the midst of it. The Lord says, 'And the day which is coming shall burn them up' (4:1).

We may not be able to detect much difference between the righteous and the wicked here. They may appear to be equally blessed and in some instances the wicked may appear to be even more blessed. But when the eternal day dawns, the difference will be plain for all to see. God says of that day:

> Then you shall again discern
> Between the righteous and the wicked,
> Between one who serves God
> And one who does not serve him
>
> (3:18).

The people of God are called, then, not to look to this life as the source of their happiness, and they are not to expect God to finally vindicate them in this life. We get into deep trouble when we expect this life to yield the things that only eternity can yield.

We are further called not to envy the wicked, but to feel deep compassion and pity for them. The happiness they enjoy in this life is all the happiness they will receive. Asaph was at first troubled by the prosperity of the wicked, but he came to see that it is utter foolishness to envy anyone who is headed for eternal destruction (Ps. 73:17-20).

The prophet Malachi was enabled by the Spirit of God to see the ultimate vindication of the righteous, but we can see even more than he did. Specifically, we are able to see the person of Jesus Christ at the very centre of the vindication of the righteous. It is only through his finished work on Calvary's cross that any are counted righteous. It should not surprise us, therefore, that the great day of vindication will find an innumerable multitude gathered round his throne and lifting up this great swelling chorus of praise to Christ:

> You are worthy to take the scroll,
> And to open its seals;
> For you were slain,
> And have redeemed us to God by your blood
> Out of every tribe and tongue and people and nation,
> And have made us kings and priests to our God;
> And we shall reign on the earth
>
> (Rev. 5:9-10).

Section IV
Promises for the journey's end

As we have already seen, the Christian is one who is on a journey. He is set on that journey by God's promises. He is sustained on that journey by God's promises. There comes a time, however, when the Christian's journey on this earth is complete. What then?

That same promising God who set the Christian on his journey and sustained him throughout has also given promises for the finishing of his race.

Because of these promises the Christian can answer the questions that have most vexed and perplexed mankind. How can one face death with tranquillity? What, if anything, lies beyond death? If there is a life beyond, what will it be like? Is death the end for the body while the soul only continues to exist?

The answers to these questions mean the Christian comes to the end of life in peace and hope. Yes, there is a natural shrinking from death for the Christian, but that shrinking is tempered by the knowledge that God has made promises regarding the future and those promises are true.

It was said of John Wesley's followers that they died well. The promises of God relating to our journey's end can enable all of us to follow their example.

25.
The promise of help in the hour of death

Isaiah 43:1-2

The people of Judah, as we have noted in previous chapters, were facing extremely harsh and trying times. Because of disobedience to God, they were destined to spend seventy years in captivity in Babylon. It was God's judgement upon them.

But even in his judgement, God does not forget to be kind to his people. In these verses, he gives them two reasons why they should not fear what was lying ahead of them.

First, they were united to him in a relationship that was unbreakable. They belonged to him. He had redeemed them and had constituted them as his people (v. 1).

Secondly, he promised to be present with them as they faced the trials and hardships of the future (v. 2).

These were not small promises. The circumstances the people were facing in Babylon would be of such a severe nature that they could be likened to passing through a deep river or walking through a scorching fire (v. 2).

God's promise to be with his people in their trials in Babylon has been precious to all the people of God who have found themselves in severe trials of one kind or another. It is a general promise that can be applied to every situation of difficulty. But this promise has also been used by Christians in a particular way — that is, to comfort themselves and others regarding death.

The swelling tide

Death can indeed be likened to a great swelling river that threatens to completely overwhelm us and sweep us away. John Bunyan's pilgrim found it to be so: 'They then addressed themselves to the water; and entering, Christian began to sink. And crying out to his good friend, Hopeful, he said, "I sink in deep waters, the billows go over my head; and all his waves go over me."'[1]

Jonah used this type of language when he was in the belly of the whale: 'All your billows and your waves passed over me... The waters encompassed me, even to my soul' (Jonah 2:3,5).

Of course, Jonah was literally surrounded by a great flood of water, but there was an inward dimension to what he was experiencing as well. That is why he talks about the waters encompassing his soul. The waters around him threatened to take his life, and the thought of death was in and of itself a mighty tide that seemed to overwhelm him.

Hymn-writers too have picked up and employed the imagery of death as the crossing of a great river. Fanny J. Crosby's hymn 'My Saviour first of all' begins:

When my life-work is ended,
And I cross the swelling tide...

Death can also be likened to walking through fire. We associate fire with pain and anguish of the most extreme kind, and that makes it a fitting image for the pain and anguish we feel when we face death.

The comforting, protecting presence

But just as the people of Judah found strong consolation and comfort in God's presence with them in Babylon, so we may find comfort regarding the hour of death in that same presence.

When David contemplated death's grim countenance, he was comforted by the presence of God:

> Yea, though I walk through the valley of the shadow
>   of death,
> I will fear no evil;
> For you are with me;
> Your rod and your staff, they comfort me
> (Ps. 23:4).

Have you ever noticed the shift that takes place in this verse? Up to this point, David has been talking *about* God, but here he begins talking *to* God. He pictures death as entering a valley (not climbing a mountain, which is extremely difficult, but walking through a valley, which is easy and pleasant). As he enters this valley a shadow falls over him (shadows in and of themselves are perfectly harmless). Suddenly he becomes aware of the fact that someone else is there. It is the very same Lord who shepherded him all through life!

This Lord, although greatly loved, had never been seen before (1 Peter 1:8), but David sees him now, and he sees him clearly enough to discern that he is carrying a rod and staff. The shepherd's rod and staff were sources of great comfort to his sheep. These instruments could be used to round up the sheep and to ward off enemies. And David, as he sees them, suddenly finds comfort flooding over his soul. He knows that as a child of God he has dreadful enemies, sworn to destroy his soul, but the sight of that rod and staff brings home the realization that he is absolutely safe; no evil power can touch him.

Many Christians, when they come to the valley of death, find themselves suddenly beset by the enemies of doubt and guilt. David would urge each of us to take our minds off those things and look for the Lord in the shadows. He is sufficient to drive away all the enemies that gather around us at the hour of death.

As we look further at the promise in Isaiah's prophecy, we discover that God not only promised to be with his people in the river and in the fire, but to keep the river and the fire from harming them in any way. That is not exactly what we would like to hear from God. We would like God to say he will arrange it so we do not have to go through the waters of trial and the fires of difficulty, and especially that we should not have to walk through that swelling tide, that scorching flame of death. But God says to the overwhelming majority of his people (only those alive at the return of Christ being exempt): 'You must go through the chilly waters of death. You must brave its scorching coals. But even though it appears to be quite ferocious, it has no real power to harm you. Its waters will not overwhelm you, and its flame will not burn you.'

The apostle Paul says essentially the same thing in his first letter to the Corinthians. There he chides death: 'O Death, where is your sting?' (1 Cor. 15:55). The Christian must still face it, but it is for him a toothless monster. Its sting has been removed.

An assuring reality

How do we know all this to be true? How do we know God's general promise to be with his people in all their times of trial, and especially in the hour of death, is reliable? How do we know his presence is sufficient to take the sting out of death?

Our God would answer that question in exactly the same words he spoke to the people of Judah:

... I have redeemed you;
I have called you by your name;
You are mine.

There is all the assurance we need. God has redeemed us from our sin at the cost of sending his own Son to endure his wrath against our sins. By virtue of Christ's redeeming work, God has established a personal, friendly, even intimate, relationship with us. He calls us by our names. By virtue of what Christ has done, God has purchased us as his own prized possession.

If God has gone to such lengths for us, why should we for a moment doubt that he will keep his promise to be present with us in the hour of death, and that his presence will be sufficient to render death quite harmless?

Safely home

Oh, by the way, Christian made it safely through. His friend Hopeful said to him, 'These troubles and distresses that you go through in these waters are no sign that God has forsaken you; but are sent to try you, whether you will call to mind that which heretofore you have received of his goodness, and live upon him in your distresses.'

Christian mused on that for a while, and then cried: '"Oh, I see him again! and he tells me, 'When thou passest through the waters, I will be with thee; and through the rivers, they shall not overflow thee'" ... Thus they got over ... also they had left their mortal garments behind them in the river; for though they went in with them, they came out without them.'[2]

26.
A cluster of promises

1 Thessalonians 4:13-18

When the Christian steps into the chilly waters of death, he finds the Lord is there to help and sustain him. Standing in the shadows of the valley of death is none other than the Good Shepherd who so tenderly shepherded him all through life. But what happens after death? The Bible provides us with answers to that question.

The first thing that happens when a Christian dies is that his or her soul goes immediately into the presence of God. The apostle Paul says, 'While we are at home in the body we are absent from the Lord' (2 Cor. 5:6). A little later he adds: 'We are confident, yes, well pleased rather to be absent from the body and to be present with the Lord' (2 Cor. 5:8).

It is clear from Paul's words that a separation takes place when the Christian dies. The body and the soul are separated from each other, with the former going into the grave and the latter going into the presence of the Lord. But what happens beyond that? Is there a future for the body, or is the grave its final destiny?

The believers in Thessalonica were so deeply concerned about this issue that they evidently put the question to Paul. His response is found in 1 Thessalonians 4:13-18. A casual glance at these verses reveals that we have here a whole cluster of promises. They are signalled by the words 'will' (vv. 14,15, 16) and 'shall' (v. 17). From these promises we can set in order a sequence or chain of events.

The return of Christ

First, the Lord Jesus Christ himself is going to descend from heaven 'with a shout, with the voice of an archangel' (v. 16). I am thankful for the emphasis supplied by that word 'himself'. It assures us that Christ's people are so exceedingly precious to him and the gathering of them is so vitally important that he will do it himself, just as the angels promised the disciples (Acts 1:9-11).

The shout and the voice of the archangel let us know that this is going to be a triumphant day.

The reunion of souls and bodies

A second link in this chain of events is conveyed by the words: 'Even so God will bring with him those who sleep in Jesus' (1 Thess. 4:14). To whom does this refer? We have already established that at the time of death the souls of believers immediately go to be with the Lord. It would seem, therefore, that those who come with Jesus when he returns are those very souls who went to be with him through the ages.

William Hendriksen observes: 'To Paul and his companions (as well as to the readers, of course) the departed ones are very real. *They are persons!* They are definitely alive and active! They are persons, moreover, whom Jesus will bring with him from heaven at his coming.'[1]

A third 'will' in these verses assures us that when the Lord returns with the souls of those believers who have died the bodies of those believers will then be raised (v. 16) and will be reunited with their souls.

The translation of living saints

That will be followed, of course, by the translation of the living (v. 17). Paul states this part of the sequence both negatively and positively. On the negative side, he says those who are alive at the coming of the Lord 'will by no means precede those who are asleep' (v. 15). Then he adds that the living 'shall be caught up together with them' (v. 16).

With these words Paul came to grips with a key part of the confusion of the Thessalonians. They had evidently reached the conclusion that Christians who died before the return of the Lord Jesus Christ were in an inferior position. Some scholars think that some of the Thessalonians may even have believed that in order to be saved it was necessary to be alive at the time of the Lord's return.

Paul's words wiped away all this confusion and concern. There is no need to be troubled about Christians who have already died. Their souls are already with the Lord, and their bodies are going to be raised first.

After the bodies of dead believers are raised, the living will be 'caught up'. Without having to pass through death, they will be instantaneously changed and will join in the air those whose bodies have been raised from the grave.

The reunion of the saints and the sight of Christ

That brings us to the final link in this chain of events, namely, the glorious convocation in the sky.

Who can imagine the sheer exhilaration and joy of meeting there in the air those beloved Christian family members and friends who preceded us in death? But the greatest glory of that moment is that we shall meet the Lord in the air' (v. 17).

Face to face with Christ, my Saviour,
Face to face — what will it be,
When with rapture I behold him,
Jesus Christ who died for me?

Face to face — oh, blissful moment!
Face to face — to see and know;
Face to face with my Redeemer,
Jesus Christ who loves me so.

Paul has one more word to add about this happy throng in the air, and that is that it will never be dispersed again. When the Lord Jesus comes to gather his saints, it is not so that he can spend a short time with them, but so that he can spend eternity with them. Paul says, 'And thus we shall always be with the Lord' (v. 17).

An unshakeable foundation

This chain of events undoubtedly sounds very fanciful and far-fetched to some. We live in a day when people can be very cool and sceptical towards the truth and very gullible and naïve about falsehood. They will walk suspiciously around truth all day and never embrace it, but will rush in and gobble falsehood down.

Make no mistake about it, these four events are not the clever inventions of a fertile imagination. Look again at this passage and you will find Paul basing all he says about the future of the believer on one solid foundation. What is that foundation? It is that 'Jesus died and rose again' (v. 14).

The believer, then, does not have to simply hang a peg in the air and try to build his hope for the future on that. His hope is built on the solid foundation of Jesus' dying and rising again. It is a sheer fact of history that Jesus came, died and rose again. That is a foundation on which one can confidently and joyfully rest.

27.
The promise of the Father's house

John 14:1-3

Jesus often spoke of his death to his disciples, but on those occasions it all seemed very distant and shadowy. On this particular night, however, it was all agonizingly real and inescapable. There was something very solemn and weighty about everything Jesus said and did on that occasion. The washing of their feet; the institution of a supper by which they were to remember his death (Luke 22:14-20); the statements that one of them would betray him and another would deny him — all of these things gave his death a strange immediacy.

Then what they had felt throughout the evening hours was clearly put into words by this one they had come to love so much: he was going to leave them (John 13:33,36).

They were shattered by it all. How could they ever go on without him? How could one of their number betray him and another deny him? What would now become of their dream that he would set up an earthly kingdom? All these questions and more crowded into their minds and battered their emotions with the force of a sledgehammer.

Troubled hearts — we know all about them, don't we? We have no hesitation in agreeing with the words of J. C. Ryle: 'Heart-trouble is the commonest thing in the world. No rank, or class, or condition is exempt from it. No bars, or bolts, or locks can keep it out.'[1]

We live in a different world from the disciples but we still feel their pain. Serious illness comes to a loved one, or to us ourselves, and our hearts are troubled. Society creaks and groans under her massive load of sin and our hearts are troubled. Loved ones die and our hearts are troubled. We live in a day in which cancer racks our bodies, tension destroys our marriages and financial hardship ruins our dreams. Ours is a day in which babies are casually discarded in hospital waste, crime ravages our streets, hunger stalks the poor and immorality parades across our television screens. And, like the disciples, we sigh and wonder and ask questions. How can such things be? How can we face another day? What does the future hold?

Thank God, Jesus did not ignore the troubled hearts of the disciples, but gave them an extended and intensive dose of comfort. Go farther into this passage and you find him assuring the disciples that his work would go on (14:12), that they would be granted power in prayer (14:13-14), that the Holy Spirit would come to help them (14:15-17) and that they would enjoy his legacy of peace (14:25-27).

This whole chapter is brimming with comfort, but none of these sayings has been more cherished than the words we have in these first three verses. There are three things we need to consider carefully in this passage.

The need to believe

First, Jesus gives in one word the cure for the troubled heart: 'Believe.' I must hasten to add, however, that Jesus was not giving them licence to believe anything they wanted. He says, 'You believe in God, believe also in me,' or, as some have translated it, 'Believe in God, believe also in me.'

These disciples already believed in God and they already believed that Jesus was God's Son and that he was, therefore, equal to God in every respect. Why, then, would Jesus urge them to believe in something, or in someone, they already believed in? The answer is that there are degrees of faith. A person can have true faith and yet that faith can be weak. The great Charles Spurgeon used to say, 'Brethren, be great believers. Little faith will bring your souls to heaven, but great faith will bring heaven to your souls.'[2] That is essentially what Jesus was saying. He was calling his disciples to believe more completely and thoroughly than they had before.

What we are dealing with here is a fundamental law of Christian living: those who have the greatest faith — who know most about the Word of God and who cling most tenaciously to it — are those who have the strongest defence against the ferocious assaults of a troubled heart.

Something to believe in

After telling the disciples to believe more firmly and strongly in God than ever before, Jesus goes on to give his disciples a specific truth for their troubled hearts to believe in. He says, 'In my Father's house are many mansions.'

I find it interesting that Jesus treated their troubled hearts by pointing them to their future home. We think the appropriate way to deal with trouble is to remove it. Because he was God in human flesh, Jesus could have done this. He could have removed the thing that was troubling their hearts. He could have refused to go to the cross and stayed with them. God is never at his wit's end when it comes to dealing with trouble. But the very thing Jesus could have done — remove what was troubling them — he refused to do. The next day he went to the cross and died. Even though he rose from the dead, he still went back to heaven and left his disciples on the earth. His cure for their troubled hearts, then, was not to remove the trouble, but to call them to look beyond it to something higher and better and nobler.

We sometimes become frustrated because we know the Lord has the power to remove our troubles, and yet he often refuses to do so. Instead, he usually does the very same thing with us that he did with those disciples. He calls us to look beyond the troubles of this life to that glorious place that awaits all the children of God.

Is your heart troubled today? Lay hold of it and soak it in the waters of this promise until the trouble is washed away. Think first about heaven as the Father's house. What a glorious thought! Heaven is the place where the Father is. So it is home. Much of what troubles our hearts in this life comes from our trying to make this world our home. We easily fall into the trap of thinking this world is our home, and if we cannot be here, heaven is the next best option. But the truth is that this world is not our home. We are strangers and pilgrims here. This world is a strange land to us.

If heaven is the Father's house, that means it is a place of plentiful provision. Our earthly fathers provide to the best of their abilities for our needs here; our heavenly Father, who has no lack of ability, will provide abundantly for us there.

If heaven is the Father's house, that means it is a place of unfailing protection. Fathers here try to protect their families, but often they are unable to do so. The heavenly Father will unerringly protect us. Nothing will be able to touch us in heaven.

If heaven is the Father's house, that means it is a place of delight and pleasure. Many of us get most of our happiness in this life from our homes, but our homes here are often tainted with misunderstanding and conflict. That home will give us perfect delight for there will be no misunderstanding or conflict there.

Then think about heaven as the place of many mansions. The word 'mansions' implies lasting dwelling-places. In this life, we live in temporary houses that are subject to all kinds of catastrophes, and we move from one place to another. In heaven we shall finally and for ever be settled.

How many mansions will there be in heaven? Enough for each child of God to have a place of his own. The greatest believers will be there, but, thank God, the feeblest saint of God will be there also. And all will be monuments to the grace of God that saved them.

Heaven is going to be wonderful! When a Christian dies, we sometimes talk as if it were a great calamity. His death may be very difficult for us, but it is certainly no calamity for him.

A reason to believe

Perhaps your response to all of this is to say, 'Yes, heaven sounds wonderful, but how can we know it's not just a pipe dream?' Jesus' disciples may have been thinking along those same lines. Thank God, Jesus also dealt with that point by telling his disciples of the certainty of this promise, or why they could believe what he was saying.

We usually make up our minds about the reliability of information we receive on the basis of the person who tells us. If it is someone we know to be given to exaggeration or deceit, we do not put much faith in what he says. If, on the other hand, we know the person to be of sterling character and unblemished integrity we believe what he tells us even though it may seem far-fetched.

When Jesus gave his disciples this promise about heaven, he rested it squarely on himself: 'If it were not so, I would have told you.' And he went on to say he would himself return and personally take them to the Father's house.

Jesus had never led them astray or deceived them in any way, but could they trust him to do such a grand thing for them?

Any lingering doubts they had about Jesus were about to be totally demolished. They were only hours away from having him snatched away from them to die on a cross. But they were also only hours away from seeing him stand before them after bursting open his own tomb!

When Jesus arose, any uncertainty the disciples had about what he had promised just melted away like dew under a blazing sun. Each probably said to himself, 'I can trust Jesus to return and to take me all the way to the Father's house just as he promised.'

28.
Promises regarding
the nature of heaven

Revelation 21:2-4; 22:3-5

One day the Christian's travelling days will be over. When that time comes the gracious God who saved him will be there to help him through death. That same Lord has promised the Christian a new body, a glorious reunion with brothers and sisters in Christ and a home in heaven.

We have already noted some aspects of what awaits the believer in heaven, but John's words in these last two chapters of the Bible give us even more details of that glorious place. The word 'glorious' seems inadequate. Heaven is going to be gloriously glorious! One glimpse of it and we shall realize the full truth of Paul's words:

Eye has not seen, nor ear heard,
Nor have entered into the heart of man
The things which God has prepared for those who love
 him

(1 Cor. 2:9).

Stunning beauty

What will make heaven such a glorious place? It will obviously be a place of stunning beauty. The Lord created this earth, and it is a place of great beauty despite being marred by sin. But its beauty will seem small compared to that of heaven.

The physical beauty of heaven will be twofold. First, there will be the beauty of the *heavenly city* itself, a beauty that John saw in his vision and recorded for us (Rev. 21:9-27). On top of that will be the beauty of the *renewed earth*. This is the part of the eternal state that we often fail to grasp. Heaven is not going to be just a huge city up in the clouds. The heavenly city, the New Jerusalem, is going to be situated on a new earth (21:1-2).

What will this new earth be like? It surely will be this present earth restored to its original beauty and glory, the beauty and glory it possessed before the ravages of sin came in. How do we know this will be the case? The word 'redemption' demands it. Redemption is God putting things back where they were, and that must include the earth being restored to what it was before sin entered.

In his letter to the Romans, Paul deals with this very matter. He says, 'Creation itself also will be delivered from the bondage of corruption into the glorious liberty of the children of God. For we know that the whole creation groans and labours with birth pangs together until now' (Rom. 8:21-22).

But heaven will be glorious, I think, not so much because of the beauty of the city dwelling on a redeemed earth, but because of what will not be there and what will be there.

Some things gloriously absent

What will not be there? John tells us in words heavy with meaning and comfort. There will be no *tears* there. Oh, how many tears there are here! But all the tears will be wiped away in heaven. And there will be no more *sorrow* there. Tears are the outward manifestation of inward sorrow. One can have sorrow, and never cry. Thank God, in heaven both the outward manifestation and the inner sorrow will be removed (Rev. 21:4).

There will be no *death* in heaven. The 'Heavenly Gazette' will not have an obituary column. There will be no mortuary on 'Glory Avenue'. There will be no cemeteries in heaven (21:4).

The reason why these things will exist no more is set out for us in the statement: 'And there shall be no more curse...' (22:3). Those words remind us that our world is now under a *curse*, and it has been almost from the dawn of human history. When God created Adam and Eve and placed them in the Garden of Eden there was no curse. All was pure, harmonious and joyful. But it did not stay that way. An intruder came in and brought the curse along with it, and that curse has been with us ever since. The name of that intruder? Sin.

Sin is rebellion against God and his law. God had given Adam and Eve one command — they were not to eat of the tree of the knowledge of good and evil. They disobeyed at that point and sin was introduced into the human race. Because God is holy, he cannot ignore sin. His very nature compels him to punish it. So he punished Adam and Eve. The primary punishment was death. The moment they sinned, Adam and Eve died spiritually; that is, they were separated from God. The harmony and communion they had enjoyed with God was gone. They did not die physically at the moment of their sin, but the seed of physical death was planted within them.

There were other punishments as well. Pain, hardship and suffering were introduced. Eve would have to bear children with pain. We should notice that her punishment was not to bear children, but to do so with pain. Similarly, Adam had the element of difficulty added to his work. Previously, his work was a joy, but now creation would resist him at every turn. So the curse of sin was, and is, pain, sorrow and death.

I find it ironic to hear so many people blaming God for all our difficulties while they still cling steadfastly to sin. God is not the source of our problems. Sin is. If you do not like the agony and suffering you see all around, turn your anger on sin, not on God. You can start by renouncing your own sins. Perhaps the greatest indication of our depravity is that we become so angry with God instead of ourselves.

That day in Eden, sin set up a rival throne against God and it has ruled like a tyrant ever since. Thank God, heaven will mean the end of the curse of sin!

Some things gloriously present

Heaven will be glorious not only because of what is not there, but also because of what, or rather who, is there.

The curse of sin is reversed only through the work of our Lord and Saviour, Jesus Christ. We can never stress this too much. So heaven is not only a place to enjoy the removal of sin's curse; it is a place for us to adore and worship the one who made it all possible. How shall we revere the Saviour in heaven? John uses three phrases to describe it.

Service

John first says, 'His servants shall serve him...' Christians appear to find it terribly difficult to serve God faithfully here and now. We tend to be haphazard, fitful and lackadaisical in our labours for the Lord. But we shall have no trouble serving the Lord in heaven. For one thing, as we have already noticed, the dragging weight of sin will be gone. But in addition to that we shall comprehend for the first time the greatness and grandeur of what the Lord has done for us. The magnificence and wonder of our salvation will so grip us that we shall be overwhelmed by it all. We take it for granted now, but then we shall realize the terrible peril sin had placed us in, how completely unworthy we were of receiving anything but condemnation, and how indescribably gracious God was to save us.

I daresay we shall not have been in heaven five seconds before we hang our heads in shame over the pitiful, petty excuses we used to avoid service.

Seeing Christ's face

John also says, ' They shall see his face…' In this life we find the words of the song to be woefully true: 'Darkness seems to hide his face.' We find ourselves nodding in agreement with Paul when he says, 'For now we see in a mirror, dimly…' (1 Cor. 13:12).

The Christian life is a continual struggle to see the face of Christ. We just get a glimpse of him, and then he is obscured by the clouds of doubt and disobedience.

Many Christians especially find his face obscured at the time of death, but after we pass over the river of death, we shall never lose sight of Christ again.

When my life-work is ended,
And I cross the swelling tide,
When the bright and glorious morning
   I shall see;

I shall know my Redeemer
When I reach the other side,
And his smile will be the first
   To welcome me.

Oh, the soul-thrilling rapture
When I view his blessed face,
And the lustre of his kindly
    Beaming eye!

How my full heart will praise him
For the mercy, love and grace
That prepared for me a mansion
    In the sky!

Bearing the character of Christ

One more thing John says: 'And his name shall be on their
foreheads.' The name of a person represents his character, and
the forehead is usually equated with visibility. Therefore, John
is saying we shall bear the character of Christ in heaven. Just
as he is holy and pure, so shall we be. We were originally made
in the image of God, but through sin that likeness was marred
and distorted. When we reach heaven the image will be
completely and permanently restored.

The promise of heaven is far too glorious to comprehend.
Our entrance there is all due to the grace of our promising God.
It was his grace that removed us from the path of destruction
and started us on the road to life. It was his grace that gave us
promises to sustain us every step of our journey. And it is grace
that will finally sweep us into the realm of heavenly glory.

Through many dangers, toils and snares,
I have already come;
'Tis grace hath brought me safe thus far,
And grace will lead me home.

Conclusion:
The heart-lift from the promises

Acts 27:20-25,42-44

What is the state of your heart? Honesty would compel many Christians to admit that their hearts are downcast and troubled.

Some would cite the difficulties of the times. Others would cite difficulties in their personal lives: a marriage gone sour; trouble with the children; financial hardship; sickness. There is no shortage of personal problems to trouble and vex our hearts.

Sadly enough, many Christians are finding difficulties even in the church. We would like to think of the church as a safe haven in this tortured world, but all too often the fellowship of our churches seems to be rife with stress, squabbling and misunderstanding.

If your strength has been sapped with the problems of life, there is good news. God has supplied his people with heart-lifting promises in the midst of difficult and trying situations.

Puritan Richard Sibbes says, 'God supports the souls and spirits of his children with promises, to arm them against temptations on the right hand and of the left...'[1]

The promises have lifted hearts in the past

Take, for example, the apostle Paul. If ever there was a man who would have been justified in being downcast and despondent, it was Paul. We find him here in this chapter a prisoner and on his way to Rome to stand trial before Caesar.

As if that was not bad enough, the ship Paul was sailing in to Rome was caught in a terrible storm. Mercilessly driven and battered by the wind, the ship was tossed from wave to wave as if it were a mere toothpick. When Paul made his appeal to Caesar he knew his life could very well come to an end at Caesar's hand, but now it looked as if he would not even get to see Caesar at all. His future was, at best, very uncertain and cloudy. How bad was this storm? Luke, the travelling companion of Paul and the author of Acts, sums it all up in one cryptic phrase: 'All hope that we would be saved was finally given up' (v. 20).

It was in the midst of this bleak situation that God gave the apostle Paul this promise: 'Do not be afraid, Paul; you must be brought before Caesar; and indeed God has granted you all those who sail with you' (v. 24).

God seems to delight in interjecting a heart-lifting promise into extremely dark and dismal situations. There was that time when the city of Samaria was surrounded by the Syrians and brought slowly and steadily to the very brink of starvation. When all appeared to be lost, God gave the prophet Elisha a promise to share with the people: the very next day food would be plentiful in the city (2 Kings 6:24 - 7:20).

Then there was that situation where Ahaz and the people of Judah were threatened by the allied forces of Syria and Israel. So bleak was the situation that the hearts of Ahaz and his people were described as being moved like the trees of the forest are moved with the wind. In the midst of that situation, God sent Isaiah to give Ahaz a clear and distinct promise (Isa. 7:1-17).

A few years later another king of Judah, Hezekiah, found himself in the midst of a vexing situation. The city of Jerusalem was surrounded by the Assyrian forces of Sennacherib.

Defeat seemed imminent. But in that situation God again sent Isaiah with the promise that the Assyrian threat would soon vanish (Isa. 37:1-7).

In each of these seemingly hopeless situations, God intervened and lifted the hearts of his people by giving them a definite promise to cling to. Such examples could be multiplied easily from the pages of Scripture.

The promises still lift hearts

Do you find yourself in a storm today? Does it seem that your situation is almost completely beyond hope? There is good news for you and your heavy heart! The God who gave heart-lifting promises to his people in the Bible does the same for his people today. No, he does not use angels to deliver his promises as he did in the case of the apostle Paul. Nor is he sending out prophets today with new words of revelation. But this does not mean God has left us in this dark world with nothing to lift our hearts. The truth is that he has filled his Word to the brim with what Simon Peter calls 'exceedingly great and precious promises' (2 Peter 1:4).

If your heart is dragging and sagging on you, what you need to do, then, is familiarize yourself with the promises of Scripture. If you are despondent over some trial, look in the Bible and see what it says about the sufficiency of God's sustaining grace. If your heart is burdened with a sense of guilt over some sin, look in God's book and see what it says about God's forgiving grace. If your heart is despondent over the militant paganism of our day, look in God's Word and see what it says about the ultimate triumph of God's cause and his people.

No matter what makes your heart ache and sag today, there is something in the book of God's promises that will comfort, strengthen, encourage and renew you. Look then, I say, in the Bible! It is all to be found here in God's book. But after you look in Scripture and find the promises of God, you must go one step further. You must believe these promises. That is the only way you will get a heart-lift from them.

Think again about the apostle Paul and his fellow-travellers in the midst of the storm. After telling his companions of the promise he had received from God, Paul adds, 'Therefore take heart, men, for I believe God that it will be just as it was told me' (v. 25).

In other words, Paul said the only way for them to find relief and comfort in the midst of the storm, the only way for them to get their hearts lifted, was to believe the promise of God. Some of those hard-bitten sailors and soldiers probably laughed when they heard Paul say an angel had appeared to him and given him a promise. Some may even have responded to his words by saying something like: 'Stupid religious fanatics! They think they know everything.'

God did not need their faith in order to keep his promise, but for as long as they refused to believe the promise of God, they doomed themselves to uncertainty and fear and deprived themselves of comfort. The only source of comfort in that stressful situation was to believe the promise of God. There was nothing else to lift their hearts.

God does not need our faith to make his promises come true. He is quite capable of keeping his promises whether we believe or not. But we need to believe God's promises to get our hearts lifted in the midst of the stresses and storms of life.

We may be sure that even though all came safely to land, they did not all come in the same way. Those who refused to believe the promise of God came safely to land after frantic hours of agitation and stress. On the other hand, those who rested in the promise of God came safely to land after hours of perfect peace that came from knowing God would not fail.

We are living in stormy, stress-filled times, but we do not have to be filled with stress. Even though there are storms aplenty all around us, we do not have to have storms within us. We can rest on the promises of God and be at peace. Ultimately, all Christians are going to come safely to land on God's eternal shore. The only question is what the journey will be like. For those Christians who make a habit of resting on God's promises, the journey will be peaceful and sweet. For those who have difficulty believing those promises, the journey will be stressful. May God himself help us each to go to heaven leaning on his precious promises.

Notes

Introduction
1. L. Berkhof, *Systematic Theology,* Wm B. Eerdmans Publishing Co., p.270.
2. Thomas Boston, *The Complete Works of Thomas Boston,* Richard Owen Roberts, Publishers, pp.469-72.
3. Robert Traill, *The Works of Robert Traill,* Banner of Truth Trust, vols iii & iv, p.37.
4. As above, p.42.
5. Richard Sibbes, *The Works of Richard Sibbes,* Banner of Truth Trust, vol. iii, p.384.
6. Charles Spurgeon, *The Metropolitan Tabernacle Pulpit,* Pilgrim Publications, vol. xlvi, p.17.

Christ and the promises — introduction
1. Traill, *Works,* p.44.
2. As above.
3. As above, pp.44-5.
4. Andrew Gray, *Works of the Rev. Andrew Gray,* Soli Deo Gloria Publications, p.131.
5. As above.
6. As above.
7. As above.

Chapter 1 — The first grand promise
1. Sibbes, *Works,* vol. iii, p.388.

Chapter 2 — Old Testament promises fulfilled by Christ
1. Josh McDowell, *Evidence That Demands a Verdict,* Campus Crusade for Christ, pp.150-74.

Chapter 4 — God's promises in Christ
1. Sibbes, *Works,* vol. iii, p.388.
2. As above, p.387.
3. As above.
4. A. A. Hodge, *Outlines of Theology,* Zondervan Publishing House, p.374.
5. Gray, *Works,* p.127.

Chapter 5 — Christ: the guarantee of God's promises
1. Jonathan Edwards, *The Works of Jonathan Edwards,* The Banner of Truth Trust, vol. i, p.541.
2. As above, p.546.

Chapter 6 — God's promise to save the believing sinner
1. John R.W. Stott, *The Cross of Christ,* InterVarsity Press, p.108.

Chapter 7 — God's promise to be the God and Father of those who believe
1. J. I. Packer, *God's Words,* Inter Varsity Press, pp.121-2.
2. William Hendriksen, *The Covenant of Grace,* Baker Book House, pp.18-19.

Chapter 9 — The promise of a present Helper
1. John Brown, *Discourses and Sayings of Our Lord,* The Banner of Truth Trust, vol. iii, p.98.
2. As above, p.104.

Chapter 10 — The promise of perseverance
1. Iain Murray, *The Forgotten Spurgeon,* The Banner of Truth Trust, p.112.

Chapter 12 — God's promise of guidance
1. Matthew Poole, *A Commentary on the Whole Bible,* MacDonald Publishing Company, vol ii, p.218.
2. Charles Bridges, *A Geneva Series Commentary: Proverbs,* The Banner of Truth Trust, p.25.

Chapter 13 — The promise of answered prayer
1. D. M. Lloyd-Jones, *Romans: Chapter 3:20-4:25,* Zondervan Publishing Company, pp.230-31.
2. William Hendriksen, *New Testament Commentary: John,* Baker Book House, p.274.

Chapter 14 — The promise of God's sustaining care
1. Derek Kidner, *Tyndale Old Testament Commentaries: Psalms 1-72,* InterVarsity Press, p.202.
2. Charles Spurgeon, *The Treasury of David,* MacDonald Publishing Company, vol. i, p.451.

Chapter 15 — The promise of perfect peace
1. Charles Spurgeon, *Metropolitan Tabernacle Pulpit,* Pilgrim Publications, vol. xxxi, p.27.
2. Albert Barnes, *Notes on the Old Testament: Isaiah,* Baker Book House, vol. i, p.406.

Chapter 16 — God's promise to meet our needs
1. Warren Wiersbe, *The Bible Exposition Commentary,* Victor Books, vol. ii, p.98.
2. Joel Gregory, *Growing Pains of the Soul,* Word Books, p.33.
3. As above, p.38.

Chapter 17 — The promise of a refuge and a strength
1. John R. W. Stott, *Favourite Psalms,* Moody Press, p.58.

Chapter 19 — The promise of forgiveness for the Christian who sins
1. David Jackman, *The Bible Speaks Today: The Message of John's Letters,* InterVarsity Press, p.30.

Chapter 20 — The promise of healing for the land
1. Matt Friedeman, 'Statistical "vital signs" show America today definitely a sick patient,' *AFA Journal,* Donald Wildmon, editor, July 1993, p.12.
2. R. V. G. Tasker, *Tyndale New Testament Commentaries, The Gospel According to Matthew,* Wm. B. Eerdmans Publishing Company, p.63.
3. John R. W. Stott, *The Bible Speaks Today: The Message of the Sermon on the Mount (Matthew 5-7),* InterVarsity Press, p.60.
4. Arnold Dallimore, *George Whitefield: The Life and Times of the Great Evangelist of the Eighteenth-Century Revival,* Cornerstone Books, vol. i, p.32.
5. S. G. DeGraaf, *Promise and Deliverance,* Presbyterian and Reformed Publishing Co., vol. ii, p.210.

Chapter 22 — Renewed strength
1. Matthew Henry, *Matthew Henry's Commentary on the Whole Bible,* Fleming H. Revell, vol. iv, p.211.

Chapter 24 — The promise of God's vindication of the righteous
1. T. V. Moore, *A Geneva Series Commentary: Zechariah, Haggai &
Malachi,* The Banner of Truth Trust, pp.167-8.

Chapter 25 — The promise of help in the hour of death
1. John Bunyan, *The Pilgrim's Progress,* Zondervan Publishing House,
p.144.
2. As above, pp.145-6.

Chapter 26 — A cluster of promises
1. William Hendriksen, *New Testament Commentary: Exposition of I and
II Thessalonians,* Baker Book House, p.113 (italics his).

Chapter 27 — The promise of the Father's house
1. J. C. Ryle, *Expository Thoughts on the Gospels, St. John,* The Baker &
Taylor Co., vol. iii, p.50.
2. Ernest W. Bacon, *Spurgeon: Heir of the Puritans,* Wm B. Eerdmans
Publishing Company, p.114.

Conclusion
1. Sibbes, *Works,* vol iii, p.384.